An Angels' Guide to Working with the Power of Light

An Angels' Guide to Working with the Power of Light

Laura Newbury

Winchester, UK
Washington, USA

First published by Sixth Books, 2011
Sixth Books is an imprint of John Hunt Publishing Ltd., Laurel House, Station Approach,
Alresford, Hants, SO24 9JH, UK
office1@o-books.net
www.o-books.com

For distributor details and how to order please visit the 'Ordering' section on our website.

ISBN: 978 1 84694 908 1

A CIP catalogue record for this book is available from the British Library.

Design: Lee Nash

Printed in the UK by CPI Antony Rowe
Printed in the USA by Offset Paperback Mfrs, Inc

CONTENTS

CONTENTS

For Robert and Thomas, and all who will live to experience the glorious times prophesied for this beautiful world.

May there be peace on Earth

Acknowledgements

I gratefully acknowledge the support given by my friends Jilly and Colin Fraser-Malcolm throughout the process of writing this book, support that sustained me in body and spirit at every stage. I thank them both for their example of living from the heart in their daily lives, and for joining me in the sending of light and prayer and practising healing with results that seemed nothing short of miraculous. I particularly thank Jilly for her creative input into the design of my book-promotion website and her heavenly meals, and Colin for his constructive comments on an early draft of the book and his help with the many technical aspects of its preparation and final submission.

I would like to thank all those who trusted and upheld me on this spiritual journey, including Jocelyn for her continual lighting of candles in prayerful support. I am particularly grateful to my sons, who naturally and easily accepted the amazing revelation of my communications with angels, encouraging me throughout with their enthusiasm and their belief in positive thinking and working with the power of light.

I acknowledge my three angels, who made their presence known to me, and all other angels who joined in, patiently dictating the chapters of this book.

Finally, I would like to thank Laura Davey, who so carefully and sensitively edited this book so as to present the angels' words exactly in the form in which they were given to me.

Preface

Dear Angels,

I thought I was an ordinary woman living in Scotland, a single parent, with the worries of all parents, such as wanting my children to be happy and to have the opportunities they deserve in education and future careers, and worries about how I can finance the lifestyle I wish for. I long for the health to be able to live a normal life, and to continue to offer my services in art teaching to those who might benefit from my experience. I fear sometimes for my future, in terms of both health and wealth.

Why have you chosen me to be your scribe? Why didn't you choose someone more confident than me to promote your teachings? I don't know how on earth I can write your book. If I were a clever person, I'd know what questions to ask, and which arguments and philosophies to bring to it. It would surely be so much better to ask someone with more brain than me. It seems such a wasted opportunity to be asking me!

***

For many years I had no particular affiliation with angels, or so I thought. I'd seen many paintings of them through my art history studies, but I tended to think they were only available to the very spiritual, to the medieval mind, or to mystics of various times and places.

I always felt my connection with spirit or the power of God most forcefully when I was out in nature – in the wilds or on a mountain – and wondered why the flowers in those remote places had such beauty.

I was aware that people from all walks of life, including children, would act out of kindness and compassion in the most unexpected circumstances. There have been countless times when I've felt unwell or in need of some kind of help and someone has come forward without being asked. I always believed there was "a power over all", to use the words of one of the Quaker founders.

The presence of angels in my life became a reality to me only very gradually, over a number of years.

My first communications with them were in writing, after a friend lent me a book in which the author suggested making a practice of writing to our guardian angels. At the time I was going through a marriage break-up involving young children, and carried a lot of guilt. I would sit late at night writing to the angels of the various people concerned on differently coloured pieces of paper, then burn the letters in the fire, or out in the garden. I didn't expect any reply, but I did feel that it helped me to focus on praying for the best outcome for everyone involved.

Some time afterwards, I lost one of my young sons in a park. As I realised he'd gone and began to panic, I felt a cry go out from my heart, asking that he'd be protected by angels until I found him. This was the very first time I was aware of specifically asking angels for help. Instantaneously, I seemed to hear someone speaking in my right ear, though it was more like a current of energy than a voice. It said, "Twenty minutes!" and I knew instinctively that I was somehow being told not to panic for that length of time – a seemingly impossible task. As I waited, I felt as if I was being pinned down by some invisible energy that was preventing me from fearing the worst. I held my other son close and focussed on finding his twin. A peacefulness surrounded us, as if we were in the eye of a storm, and I was very aware of the connection between us, and between the two separated children.

I didn't know at that time that focussing on the best outcome, and sending out light or love from the heart, rather than panicking, was the best thing I could possibly have done. I continue this practice to this day for my friends, or for any situation that needs a prayer, and sometimes my close friends or my sons join me in doing this. Often we have the experience of being held by some invisible force, and of time standing still.

When my son was found, on the river bank, there was a circle of unknown children standing silently round him a short distance away, as if protecting him, without speaking to or touching him, so that he was totally unaware of them. They were very young, but an older boy on a bike was cycling up to every passer-by to ask if they had lost him. I wondered years later if they were angels. The incident happened at Dunblane, where there had been the terrible shootings of children a few months previously.

I held the experience in my heart, and didn't ask the angels in that way again until many years later, when I was once more in a crisis.

I'd been unwell for some time with continual debilitating headaches day and night. During this time, one of my sons also became very ill and unable to eat. There were visits to doctors and to the school, hospital appointments to no avail, and seemingly endless waiting for results. I became totally despondent, and was in great fear. Pacing the floor one night, I experienced again a rush of motivating energy with the realisation that there *was* something I could do! I thought, "If they came to help the child all those years ago, they'll come again!"

I hurriedly lit a candle in the pink glass holder that I now always use when writing to the angels, grabbed a pen, sat down at the kitchen table, and wrote an SOS: "Are you out there? Can you help?" Immediately I found myself scribbling an answer. I kept the original piece of paper:

If you believe it, then ask us. We can help him, and you – you are loved. He will be fine, and so will you. Speak up about him. We are here and can only help when you ask. All is well. You will be healed. Troubles will vanish. Only believe. There is a red angel for him. Blue for you.

A series of apparent coincidences led to our finding a specialist who understood the problem. My son's healing was quite dramatic, finally surprising even the doctors. He wasn't on medication for long, and became completely well, as he is to this day.

***

My own healing took longer than my son's, and some of the process is recorded in this book. It was mostly done through forgiveness, and learning to use white light through the power of imagination.

I wasn't new to the concept of healing pain through forgiveness, having for years been inspired by the teachings of Louise L. Hay, whose influence I'd like to acknowledge. If I could take only one book to a desert island, it would be one of hers. The angels helped me to put into practice these same concepts.

I often went back to thank them for their help, writing on scraps of paper and sticking them around the kitchen, because I couldn't think what else to do with them. If I was outside I wrote in snow, in sand on beaches, or in any other way I could think of. It seemed a bit silly, as I knew the angels would receive the message anyway, but I felt the need to acknowledge their help in this way.

Each time I sat down to thank them, there was a new message, and these I began to collect into an envelope. I was still having dreadful headaches, and was often afraid of going somewhere alone, blacking out, and not being able to get home. I started to ask for help continually in order to cope with everyday things.

They kept saying, "It is time!" I didn't know what that meant, but every time I looked at a clock it seemed to be at, or to have stopped at, 11:11. Then the message came:

It is to pass and we are guiding you. You will know what to

do – and it will be in right timing. Watch the clocks and how they change speed, for the Earth time is shaking free, and celestial time is to become real on Earth. All is well.

The pain is to show you how to clear the way for a better life where everything for your highest good manifests quickly. The pain has been your teacher. Joy and service are to come together in your life. Until now they have been separate and service has been your duty. But now it is with great joy that what you most desire to do is also of great service to mankind. Believe it and do it.

I scored out "mankind" in the message and substituted "people", but the word "mankind" came back insistently until I reinstated it. Since then I've never attempted to change any of the angels' words.

How was I possibly in a position to serve mankind? I was unwell and had little confidence and very limited financial means. I'd go to the window and ask for a sign or for something to help me understand, and almost every time a rainbow would appear. I saw rainbows in the most extraordinary situations, such as in a summer sky above me as I lay on a beach. Once when I was thinking about this phenomenon in the bathroom, the sun came out and caught the edge of the bathroom mirror, casting a beautiful rainbow right across the floor. I have a terrible habit of trying to analyse everything, and I think this was the angels' joke, to catch me off guard as it were.

I asked, "Please tell me the meaning of the rainbows."

This is our communication to you to show you that we are here. The rainbow symbols are a bridge between the physical and the non-physical realm – yes, in reality you see it, but the symbolic meaning is there also.

"Well, what am I supposed to do with the bridge?"

Go over it whilst staying in the physical – it is to remind you that the earthly life is only a parallel existence to the heavenly one, which you are also living from your physical self, and that this can be accessed, and affected by what you are doing in your earthly life. You only need to connect – by doing this you are helping the world to evolve. We need you.

I finally asked a close friend for help over the messages I was receiving. Hearing my story, she immediately made an appointment for us to see a healer in Fife who could channel the angels. We set off by car, laughing and giggling, as it was such a beautiful day and we rarely had the opportunity to go off on trips together. Then the most extraordinary thing happened.

We were turning off just after the Forth Road Bridge in heavy traffic when white things in huge numbers started to come across the windscreen. At first I thought it was polystyrene pieces that had fallen off a passing lorry, but my friend was crying, "Feathers! Feathers!" They came so thickly that it was amazing she could see to drive, like being in a snow blizzard on a beautiful sunny day. Yet somehow they never obscured her vision. "Get one! Get one!" I tried to open the passenger window, but it wouldn't budge. The feathers stopped and the window began to open. Then the window stuck again and the feathers once more came across in force. I tried to see where they were coming from. It was as if there was a hole in the sky somewhere up on our right and someone was shaking out a giant pillowcase. They must have continued to fall for around five minutes. Feathers of all sizes.

To this day I can hardly believe what we saw, but I know that the angels had finally given us the physical manifestation of feathers as a sign of their presence, and as confirmation that they were the authors of the messages I'd been receiving, and the co-ordinators of the events that had led me to the point of writing this book.

***

And so my channelling of the angels' messages began. I have friends who can channel, but I don't know how they do it. I can only describe how I have done it.

The process was always the same. I would light a candle, sit down at my computer, type the words "Dear Angels", usually followed by a question, and wait, my fingers resting on the keyboard. The angels' words came one at a time: I never knew what the whole sentence would be. As I was typing, I felt that the sentences couldn't possibly be making sense. When I got to the end of the paragraph, I would sometimes read back over what I'd written and be amazed to find that not only the sentence made sense but the whole paragraph.

Usually I had to write as fast as I could to keep up, as the words came like thoughts. Some of the words used by the angels were unfamiliar to me, and I had to look them up afterwards. Some were old-fashioned, and yet perfect, and seemed chosen very specifically, so I made no attempt to modernise them.

When the words ceased to come I would type another question, and as I did an answer would again begin to form, word by word. When I felt that a communication on a particular subject had finished, I would type, "Thank you, Angels".

At first I couldn't write much. I was still having a lot of pain, and would often start to feel dizzy or nauseous, or very sleepy, and would have to walk away from the computer. I was told by the angels that this was because of the high "vibration" at which they operate. Somehow I was having to reach up to that level, while they had to come down to mine. I think the purpose of lighting candles and of prayer is to form a bridge from where we are to where they are, to aid communication.

I gradually became aware of three different styles of speech, which are the voices of the three angels Amber, Uriel and Ariel, whom I've come to understand are with me continually, helping in my personal life when I ask. These are the angels who dictated most of the script to me. Other angels have made their identity known. Often Archangels Raphael and Chamuel offer guidance, and occasionally Archangels Michael, Gabriel and Sandalphon. As with my own accompanying angels, they tend to "speak" according to the subject matter, so that, for instance, Raphael speaks on the subject of healing, Chamuel on unconditional love, and Michael on the casting out of fear and negativity. Because healing requires casting out fear, forgiving and letting go of the past, and letting love come into one's life, these angels seem to be working interdependently. Sandalphon speaks on music and the vibration that connects us with the divine, and Gabriel on purification. There may be others. The angels always speak collectively as "we", even if I've addressed a question to one of them in particular, but I'd imagine they are always speaking collectively the message from God, so it would be the same whoever the messenger was. They have no self-interest or ego as it were.

Often it's as if I can feel them laughing, or I think of a question and their answer comes as a joke that makes me laugh out loud. They seem merry, and I'm a hundred per cent certain of their sense of humour and fun.

***

It was very soon made clear to me that our communications were to form a book. I asked the angels many times if I was the right person to undertake this task, as I didn't feel I had the authority to write such a work. It was as if on one level I was fully trusting, waiting for their words, but on another I was trying to analyse it all, and unable to take in the implications of what was happening to me. I gave them a very hard time, and became amazed at their patience with me.

It was also made clear to me that in presenting our

communications as a book nothing was to be changed, and I knew I had to trust that.

The only words of the original script that I omitted were those in which the angels had given me a personal direction. If I was too tired, for instance, they would say, "You are going to sleep!" which was a signal that I should stop, or if I started to worry over what I was writing, I'd be told, "Don't analyse!" They would even make me laugh out loud with these unexpected comments.

Having taken out these directions, I needed to organise the dialogue in some way. I realised it fell very clearly into sections on different subjects, such as "forgiveness and trust" or "letting fear go", which I therefore made into chapter headings. I made a few changes to the sequence of these chapters, and moved a number of communications from one chapter to another, according to subject matter.

Such changes were necessary only in the early part of the book, however. When I began to take down the angels' messages, I had no idea of the emerging themes or where the dialogue was heading. The communications had sometimes been very short, and often related to more than one subject. In time, sessions became longer and the dialogue flowed more continuously. Thus the later chapters of the book were each written at a single sitting, and here it was necessary only to add the chapter titles.

Within chapters I omitted my "Dear Angels" and "Thank you, Angels" from the beginning and end of each communication, for ease of reading, using them only to open and close the chapter itself. Where such an omission created a hiatus in the dialogue, I made the break explicit with a row of asterisks.

The title of the book came to me unexpectedly from one of my teenage sons. It was as if his angel spoke through him. When I admitted to my sons that I was writing a book, they were intrigued to know what it was about, but I told them I couldn't reveal that until it was finished. Then one of them said, "I know! It's about working with the power of light and asking the angels.

Go for it, mum! It's what you know about!" For a moment I thought they must have found my manuscript, but they assured me they hadn't. "We know you better than you think!" They told me that they'd seen the changes in me, and how I'd become well and so much more positive. They'd seen the candles burning and knew about light-sending, and remembered how I'd reminded them to ask the angels for help and protection.

I was surprised to realise that in writing this book I'd been using language which some might recognise as biblical, even though it was never my intention to write a religious book. During my formative years I'd been involved with Quakers, and the aspects of Quaker practice that were most important to me were the waiting in silence to be guided by spirit and living truthfully. But by the time of my first communications with angels I hadn't attended a Quaker Meeting for many years, and had scant knowledge of other denominations. The angels who gave me the words of this book made it very clear that they are not affiliated with any culture or religious denomination. Although they communicate with us, they are beyond our world, with powers beyond our understanding, but the power that connects them with us comes from love. Love is universal, and as the angels say, "Love is the only real power there is."

I therefore trust that readers of this book will be able to see beyond the limitations of the language I've worked in, and feel the inspiration of the angels who have given me their loving guidance, which I now offer to you.

Chapter 1

The Beginning

Dear Angels,

May I ask you to help me with the protection of my communications with you?

Do not fear. We are taking care of this. By lighting the candle, it is as you felt – that the light of that one flame was enough to keep you safe. Continue this. We are here and will guide you, and you need not fear.

We love you all, and take great delight in communicating on things both great and apparently small, but nothing is too small for us angels, and we urge you to keep asking, for our power to help is unlimited, and you are not "being greedy" or taking another person's share by asking us. This is limited human thinking. As long as you keep a loving heart, and have the good of all the world as your aspiration, then nothing can be too small or big to ask.

Surely I can't be making this up?

We laugh at your surprise at yourself – did you think that you would be led to use such vocabulary as ours? We adapt what we say so that you can understand its meaning, but the essence of what we say is ours for you to channel. You hear our words and translate them, but some phrases are better left in "angelspeak". This is also to help you know what is coming from us and what is yours.

My heart sings. Thank you for bringing me home to the light!

You have transformed and will lead others to do this. We shall assign to you certain tasks and you will know what to do – it is not time yet, but very soon. All is well! Keep shining and you will not fall again, for everything comes together for good for those who willingly seek the light, and you have received our blessing, as a beloved child of God and of the light, for it is as it is written in the book – all is coming to pass and the world is transforming even at this moment. We need you for the light – you can do much to help. Fear not. We are with you and constantly guide you, now and always, and the world will rejoice for salvation is coming through the transformations of those whose hearts are open and who carry out their mission on Earth, and are unbending in their search for the truth, and in reaching their full potential. Forever and forever the world will continue to turn, and the axis of the Earth shall be based on love and joy, and not fear, for this is written in our book. So fear not, for we hold you dear, as we do all those who bravely pioneer the path of light.

What is this book you speak of?

The Book of the End of Times – it is not as you fear, though, for it is the record not only of the evil of the world, but also of the world's awakening to the light, and of the new time which is not yet recorded but which will be dependent on the outcome of the transformation which is already taking place. So the pages are being written now – this has only been dreamed of, but now comes to pass. We angels work tirelessly for the good of mankind, but can only help the world (Earth) by assisting the evolution of people on Earth, and time is short, and we urge those who are aware to move fast, to bring about the kingdom of God, as it is written.

***

I'm here if you want to speak.

We ask that you type. It is unveiling – the truth. Not all will survive this time ahead, but our message is that those who stay must not fear. Only love can survive the changes. This means to live your life amid massive changes – and these will take place, daily. You will not be able to tell whose hearts are ready, so do not question. It is a personal decision for all. You must not fear. This is our main instruction to you. All is well. We will guide many through this time, but can only work through the hearts on Earth of those who are willing to receive the light, and you are one. That is why we communicate with you. We ask that you hold the light in your heart, and this will strengthen our communication to you, and make it possible to reach more.

Thank you, Angels. Is there anything more?

The great peace of God is present on Earth. We hold the light as a way forward for the peoples of the Earth to reach that peace, whilst still in the physical realm. This has been done by the mystics of all faiths, but will now be achieved by ordinary souls and children too. Some will lead the way. These are blessed times, which have been prophesied, but which continue beyond the prophecies.

You knew when you were young, and read your Bible, that you could be living in the times of the Apocalypse, but then none knew of the possibility of survival. Now we know that there is a way through, and that Heaven and Earth can connect. For mankind can be lifted up as one heart connects with the next. And so it shall be.

There is so much written about the 11:11 phenomenon and its meaning, by all kinds of psychics, that I feel out of my depth in writing about this subject. But I know that you are leading me and that there must be something I can add to the knowledge already received. I await your guidance.

You are to tell the world how to transcend, and to teach this in practice, and we will guide you when the time is right. The children need to know what to do and you can help them, for you are a natural teacher and they will listen to you. This is not a posting on the internet but a practical guide.

***

[*On Easter Day 2006 I received the following message.*]

We rejoice. The Earth is surrounded by angelic forces. Many angels are present and you will experience acts of kindness daily by all you meet. All is well, and many hearts on Earth are linked together to bring light into the darkness of the world. We are constantly amazed by the light and the power of the human heart, and many shall be saved by their faith. By holding the light in your heart, you build bridges for us to cross, and we can reach you in the physical. As the forces of good shall unite and rise to yet higher levels, so shall the forces of evil fight back. They are ultimately less than the light but are nevertheless powerful and can hold sway where fear abounds. It is why we say to you that all who work for the light must not fear. That in itself is your power, which renders it impossible for the dark powers to operate. This negation of fear requires faith, especially when fear is all around. We believe it possible, though, and we will be beside all who are resisting evil. This can only be done person by person, not by government or institution.

Are you still here?

Be of good faith and practise taking down our words. Fear not that it is beyond you to carry out this work. Faith is all that is necessary, and we will impart the knowledge to you.

But I don't feel that my faith is very great compared to that of many others.

Be that as it may, your faith has made you whole and you are perceptive, and will not allow ego or any false beliefs to outweigh what you feel to be God's will. This is why we assign this task to you, for you cannot be corrupted where the truth is concerned. "But" is no longer a relevant word here – let it go now.

Thank you, Angels. I am blessed.

Chapter 2

The Importance of Living from the Heart

Dear Angels,

You want to ask us how to discern when a feeling is coming from the heart.

You read my mind.

We tell you to forget trying to work it all out from the mind. It is imperative that you follow your hearts. This is where the true power comes from. Truth comes from the heart. That is why you ask your heart whether something is true, is it not? The truth may differ from person to person, but the important fact is that a person must follow his own truth from his own heart. Then all difficulties fall away and his life will move forward easily. He will receive all the help he needs and no one will dispute him, unless the intention of the other person is to lie and betray. That other will recognise that the truth is being spoken and followed. Then he in turn has a decision to make as to whether to follow that example.

Regarding whether the thought is from the heart, the corresponding feeling is sometimes powerful, sometimes very tiny but insistent, repeating itself until a person takes heed of it. It is often humorous, or contrary to the solution created by the mind, "deceptively" simple (but not deceptive), risky, amazing, very creative, promoting a sense of freedom and happiness.

From the mind the feeling is more of seriousness, heaviness, compromise which includes loss of something integral to the situation being decided about. Intuition comes very quickly without any thought – in a flash. It comes neither from mind nor from heart, but straight from source.

People are now coming to the understanding that the heart is a power, and that it possesses its own "intelligence". The mind is the tool of the heart, as the computer is the tool of the thinking person who operates it. The heart is the centre of love, the test of truth, the motivation for forgiveness, trust and gratitude, and the perceiver of beauty and truth. Joy is a reward felt in the heart, and tears come from the heart, and can be born of joy and sorrow. The heart can be gladdened or saddened or all of a flutter, or it may sing and be light or feel cold and heavy. The heart can be at peace or in the mouth, or on a string or given away or broken, set on fire, rekindled, mended and enlarged, and connected (and we shall elaborate on this later in the text). Who or what motivates the heart? It is your connection with the divine, and you cannot live or die without it for you are all from the divine source: every one of you.

If love is from the heart, or if the heart is the centre of love, what about fear?

Fear is born of the mind, and does not exist outside the mind. It is illusion, and can be cast out. Love is real, and cannot be extinguished – ever. It is what you are made of, and it is integral to all matter within and outwith the universe. It is a power, as we have said. It is the power which has sent you on your journey through the ages, and to which you shall return. It is your home. We call you home, and we guide you home at all times. Be reassured that the journey is always to love. Love is the destination, though the journey is infinite.

You are saying that love is the only power there is, but you also speak of the power of the mind. Can you explain this further?

The power of the mind is beyond your imagination. You have no idea of the power of your mind. It is a creative power which attracts situations to you, and manifestations in the physical realm, in accordance with the beliefs which you currently hold. The mind runs on the power, but is not the origin of the power. It "taps" into the power of the universe, in the way a computer plugs into the socket.

***

I feel like writing a short piece. Do you have something for me?

You wish to understand how the power of the human heart is perpetuated, and transformed into a power for healing. It is the feelings of joy and gratitude and appreciation that hold the power and create more. Joy is the reward for the heart, motivating a person to feel the gratitude and appreciation. Gratitude is a form of prayer, as we have said, and appreciation is recognition from the heart of all that is truly from source. Appreciation is the highest quality of all.

***

I'm here at last.

Dawn is breaking even now on your planet. This is the new dawn of a new age. You are all creating a new place to be, and the possibility of a "peaceable kingdom" is here at last. It is in your hands. We angels can only uphold that vision of peace and support you in your actions. People are now coming to the understanding that the human heart has its own intelligence. Yes, people have known this for many ages, but your scientists are now able to support and "prove" this knowledge, and there is to be a massive awakening of heart energy as knowledge of this becomes widespread. We laugh. Why is it necessary to "prove" in order for people to "believe"? But that is the way of your world – until these new times. So, will that make it any easier for people to follow their hearts and act on that true guidance from within which is available to you all? There will be those who will strive even to corrupt this new information – even to corrupt what cannot be corrupted. So it will be even more necessary to seek within to find and follow the truth of your hearts: your hearts, and not anyone else's.

Chaos will become normal, and those of you who hold the light for others to see by are asked to stand firm and hold your light steady. We ask that you raise your vibration by magnifying the light that you already hold. (Do this in your imagination and it will be so.) And fear not.

Thank you, Angels. Who's speaking, please?

Chamuel – yes, you are surprised, but who other than I when the subject is about heart.

Hearts are huge powerhouses of love energy, which heal and dissolve pain and show the way of truth and peace. They are not only those physical organs, or the red symbols on your valentine cards! And what are those physical organs which pump blood? Blood is the life flow, the joy moving in your body. Without this life within, you of course cannot exist in your physical body.

Thank you, Chamuel.
I get very frustrated about this "heart" business – for example, how to know when I'm coming from the heart.

Stop right there and tell us if you are speaking the truth. You know that is not true. You know very well when you are coming from the heart, because of the *feeling* that accompanies it. We think what you are trying to say is that you have been so well trained to revere the mind, and clever thinking and logical argument, and have for so long held the belief that will-power is a good thing, that it comes as a shock to realise that there is an easier way – the way that was natural to you all along. Of course clever thinking and will-power can be very good things if you put the heart foremost, and make your mind work for your heart. Then success in all things is guaranteed.

A lot of people believe it to be the other way round.

Who does?

I have believed it, for one. But I now realise this has been to my detriment. I've sometimes been afraid of "coming from the heart" for fear of seeming weak or naïve, or of being hurt, criticised or ridiculed.

Unfortunately there are many like you who have acted and spoken from the heart and had these negative experiences, as you often have. These experiences have closed you down and blocked you even from seeing your own truth at times. (Many children have been blocked in this way, as they have grown up and learned how to charm and deceive.) Now you have "seen the light" and have lost your fear about speaking your truth because you know that it cannot be disputed, and that anyone who mocks is merely mocking himself. Unfortunately there are in your society whole systems built around false values and in which it is imperative to be good at lying. However, most people are not taken in by this. They can discern what is true. But they accept the lies as normal – as the only way to survive in these institutions. This is exacerbated by seeing examples of people who step out of line, or tell the truth, being punished. Again it is fear that motivates people to punish, and fear that stops them from stepping out of line themselves. It is the letting go of the fear that allows a person to step out of line. He may be held up as an example of a loser, but ultimately he is the winner.

What of people who are tortured or killed or forced to see their families suffer to make them into an example?

They are the winners though they may lose their lives, and they know it and so do their tormentors. You have heard this before.

Yes, I'd have to search for it in the Bible.

***

I'm here to take down your words. I'm finding this hard to understand. I need to focus more, I think. Does the heart hold its own power, then, independently of the conscious mind?

We are here and we guide you in this writing, so take down our words and trust that you are hearing us.

Yes, the heart has its own power, and that is because it connects with source. It is the chakra that connects with the divine and that holds that part of you which is divine. However, it needs the mind to be in harmony for its perfect operation. If the mind is in opposition to the heart, then the body system becomes open to disease and pain. You have experienced this.

Yes, though I'd no idea what was happening, and didn't know that my mind was going in a different direction from my heart.

Bad feelings and bad sensations are the guidance that tells you there is something going wrong. Often you assumed they were there because *you* were wrong, and used your will-power to force yourself to do things that did not feel right. This was because of the programming you received from early childhood, from school and society. It is learned behaviour, much of which is in place to protect you so that you can exist at ease in your society, and be accepted.

But wouldn't there be mayhem if we didn't "toe the line" but did exactly as we wanted all the time? Wouldn't there be complete anarchy?

There *is* mayhem. There *is* anarchy, and it is spiralling out of control. This is because of the lies, the corruption, which stem from societies that did not allow their children to follow the way of the heart. They delude themselves and sell their lies to their people. The corruption is everywhere. It is in the media. It even exists as poison in the Earth and seas, and in the food you eat and the air you breathe. It is a cancer which has spread from generation to generation, and now those who wield the greatest power have built their false towers so high that they can only fall. And fall they will. Anyone who cares to see can see this. Children know it and are rebelling in every way they can.

Everyone is asking, "What has happened to our society and to our children?" Your children are part of the great scream of the Earth in its death throes, malfunctioning and choked with poison.

It is time. It is time. It is time, and the universe calls for termination.

Then adults and children will cease to walk around thinking, "What is the point?" (of caring, of respecting), for they will be fighting for their lives, and for life itself, and saving themselves will become part of the saving of the Earth. They will fight with their hearts, and their motivation will be for the saving of themselves and of the planet. Caring and respect for the Earth and its peoples, and for all life, will be the great motivation which will lift everyone and everything to a new way of being, and to salvation.

Will the "false towers" of those who currently wield world power have to fall before this change can come about?

Yes, though many of you are preparing the way, and you are one. By writing this book, and by living and recording your transformation to full awareness, you are showing the way. Many on this Earth are "lightworkers" and "wayshowers".

I don't know the way, or what to do.

You are "doing it as you go along".

The same way as I'm writing this book?

Yes.

Thank you for your communication.

We thank you for your perseverance.

***

What about horrific situations of suffering, and pain and ugliness and evil? How can you say that there is light and love within these situations?

We applaud you for your honesty and sense your anger. God's love is indeed everywhere. It is the disconnection of the human soul from its source that causes the suffering, pain, horror and ugliness. The source is always there, though. You could think of it as electricity which is there but not seen or felt because the plug has been pulled out.

I understand, but I'm having a problem with the knock-on effects from situations where people have become disconnected, and where their actions affect innocent people. An extreme example would be an area polluted by chemicals, maybe through war, where people can't get enough food. It's not their fault that they are starving. It's not they who are disconnected, but those who caused the pollution, surely?

We really wish that you learn to type, as your thought-forms are too fast for your typing speed, and it is interrupting the flow. We are operating at a much higher frequency and it is making it hard work for you to connect.

On your question, we have to tell you that the people who are suffering have, on an unconscious level, put themselves in that situation. They have been born to encounter that situation for their soul's progression. Yes, we know you are sending out indignant thought-forms, but bear with us.

The purpose for their lives is the journey towards love. Those who are suffering most are in effect helping those who have perpetrated the horrific events to learn to love ultimately. This may have been the contract agreed before they incarnated on Earth.

However, there was never an original contract which required that people suffer. You were designed to live in happiness and joy and to have everything you wished, including health. Illness and pain were the exception. It should have been possible for man to manifest a life of happiness and well-being. Your bodies were designed to heal, and even death should have been an easy process. It is through the choices man made that evil came to reside on Earth and to infiltrate his very consciousness. This created consequences. The consequences have had to be lived out. This we call karma.

Earth is now so depleted of resources that it struggles to heal itself and to support life. Not just human life, but all life. Now people must make huge efforts to heal themselves and release their karma. There is no time left, as we said at the beginning of this book, to create more negative karma.

Thank you. Who has been speaking, please?

It is I, Uriel.

***

I'm here to continue writing.

All is in right timing. All patterns will unfold and reveal themselves. All of creation is constantly evolving, in response to the greater rhythm of the spheres. The human heartbeat is connected with this rhythm. Human life must evolve with the Earth because it is connected with the Earth, as well as being connected with the divine source. Earth is at this time being bombarded with energies from a higher source, in order that it will raise its vibration to a much higher level. Many people are sensing this, and are feeling displaced and exhausted as a result. It is a time of transition for everything that lives. Human life is not exempt.

So now all must be resolved and healed, and all people must follow the path they came on Earth to tread. Follow your hearts, and seek the truth in all things – your truth, not anyone else's truth. By following your hearts you will be creating the new world. Heaven shall reign on Earth, and Earth shall be a reflection of Heaven. These are glorious times, which have been prophesied but which will continue even beyond the prophecies.

You have spoken of the importance of following the heart, of seeking the truth, of forgiving everything and healing all pain, of prayer, of the importance of sensing the beauty in things, and of feeling gratitude and appreciation and respect for all living things.

Yes, and of feeling compassion for others. This is important.

As we said before, living continuously in this way, and seeking the joy, will attract more to you, for joy is the reward of the heart which is pure in its intention to follow the light. By this we mean all that is mentioned above – the desire to follow the light, to forgive and heal, and to seek truth and beauty in all things, to know compassion – to desire to do all these things, not out of fear of punishment if you stray off that path, but because it is the way which is truly natural to you, and which brings the reward of well-being, and further joy.

It is to be like the tree which bends and sways in the wind, but resists not, and forever grows towards the light, and bears its leaves and its flowers and fruits in season, and shelters and provides nourishment for millions of creatures, and grows beautifully, shaped by the weathers, and is all the more beautiful as it bears its scars as ornaments which enhance its appearance. For the tree knows how to stay in the light, and grow with the light, and the many animals it shelters also live with wondrous acceptance of their circumstances. But only man has learned how to deviate from the true way of living, through greed.

It is good to have free will, but there is now no more time for the effects of man's evil intention to heal, and the time for releasing karma is short, for the universe cannot any longer support anything which was born of fear. Free will is the last gift that people on Earth have experienced. Henceforth, in future times, man will not have the opportunities to stray far from the light, and if he does, then his deeds will not affect others.

People who live in the light will have learned to protect themselves from anything which is not for their highest good. Their vibration will be too high for the darkness to penetrate, as one candle in pitch darkness can be seen for three miles, and not engulfed by the darkness around it, whereas the darkness around it is totally dissolved by the light of the one candle. This is why we say to you that anything which is not for the light will be swept away. It will be too bright for the perpetrators of evil to see. Already it is becoming too bright for some of them to continue to carry out their mission.

There is a fire raging across the planet. It is the fire kindled by the people who are shining their light, and joining together in their mission to save the Earth. Anyone, anywhere, who prays for anyone or anything is augmenting this fire. We can see it because it now burns so brightly, and cannot be put out. We rejoice that the possibility of the Earth and its people being saved is now here, because of those of you who have desired to work for the light.

Dear child, we are with you, and with all who are on this path, and we work tirelessly beside you. We remind you to ask for our help on matters of the greatest and smallest importance, for we cannot help unless you ask, or someone else requests your help, through prayer. So pray for one another, or send out the white light, continuously if you can, to all situations.

Thank you, Angels.

Chapter 3

Healing from the Heart

Dear Angels,

Are you here?

We are ever present, and we have been calling you to your writing. We are happy that you are here.

You are learning about the healing power of love, and how forgiveness is the key to set the healing process in motion. You are now understanding how pain in the body is a signal from the brain to the heart that something needs to be addressed, and healed. The process always starts in the mind as a belief or a thought, and it can take many years for the body to process the thought or belief as pain. Pain is the final result of this process, but is the beginning of the journey of healing, which ultimately leads back to the mind and to the changing of thoughts and beliefs (to the "change of mind"), and the response in the physical body is then to cast out the pain and heal. Even an accident started with a thought which was off track, though you may not have been aware of the thought in your conscious mind.

I understand what you are saying, about feelings holding the key to creating joy and healing, but how does a person get into that space of joy and appreciation in order to create more if, for instance, he's in a state of depression. If he's too "down" to feel, no matter how much he longs for happiness and to feel good it seems impossible to reach that place. Can you advise?

You must understand that these negative feelings are illusion, and that it is necessary to break free from them. We understand that this seems like an impossibility, as you have said, but know that it is possible. Call on us for help. Trick your mind into a state of happiness by acting as if you were happy, until finally you find that the illusion is broken and you are out into the light. Movement and dance, good company and laughter, thinking of the people you love and the things you love doing, lighting candles or being in natural light, in nature, sensing, touching, taking into your body the perfumes and aromas of nature, feeling the wind, seeing colours change in the light. These are more real than your negative illusion, as they come from the love which is real, and have the power to transform you, and they will. They are gifts to your soul. Do not worry about being depressed. We know this sounds like a contradiction, but if you make any move to get out of it, you will find that there is help, and you can build yourself higher with each step forward. Again we say to you that you can use white light to dispel the depression, as with fear. This will work. Use your imagination to visualise the light and see it enter your body, healing and dissolving the darkness. You know that it is your imagination that has created the darkness, so it is just as possible for your imagination to take you back to the light, no matter how far you have fallen. Trust. And believe our words. Many sensitive people are struggling with depression, for they take on the burdens of the world they are in. It is time for them to realise the light which will take them to joy, and that this is more real than the darkness. All are forgiven, and all deserve to access their greater good, and to reach that place of light, which is real.

What about the example of, say, a footballer who may expect to receive an injury at any time just because of the nature of his sport? Does he on a subconscious level attract the situation for the injury to occur?

Yes. The accident holds a purpose which may have effects well beyond the game where the accident occurred. There may be a reason why he must be out of the game for a time, perhaps to review his life, or to let someone else take his position for a time so that the other person can learn what he needs to. Even a small insubstantial injury happens for a purpose. It may be a delicate shift of the body's awareness which is to affect the greater development of awareness and ultimately of soul. It is in the physical that the "game" (of life) is played out, but the players are the heart and the mind, and the outcome will affect the soul.

We understand that you may find it hard to understand that even the smallest events have a purpose. Everything has its purpose. Every action creates an effect which affects firstly yourself and then others.

May I ask about pain and its purpose? I mean physical pain. Why must we suffer?

It is all the same. It matters not whether it is physical or mental pain. It is all part of the process of soul going off centre and coming back to centre – of illness and healing. You live in the physical body and it cannot be any other way. The pain is the signal from the physical body to let you know that there is something wrong, and the greater the pain, of course, the greater the need to correct your path.

If the signals are ignored, the pain will ultimately break out in greater force at a later time, as illness, and the healing will be a more complex process, especially if the pain has manifested in areas related to but further from the initial source of the problem. The original source of the pain is always mental – mental pain. Yes, even in the case of a small knock or bump or bruise. You do not have to believe this yet but you will. However, given the right timing, place and circumstances, all can be resolved and healed, and it is never too late to heal. We must emphasise that miracles of healing can and do occur, and will become more common as man expands his belief in the power of his mind. For example, there are more people now able to reverse an illness such as cancer without any medical intervention of the conventional kind. You have met such people. There are others whom you have heard of but not met who have regrown parts of their bodies.

But how is this done?

You are largely unaware that your body knows how to heal, and is healing, repairing, growing and evolving all the time, without the need of the awareness of the mind to guide it in any way.

Is it working on heart power?

Yes, in a way it is, though it is not that you are in any way conscious of the function of your heart in this process, whereas there are other functions of your heart of which you are very much aware.

When you feel ill or experience pain, it is because your body has signalled to your consciousness that something is wrong. You must then set your mind to work to find the solution, and begin the healing process. This is a slow process when operated through the mind, as you well know, because the mind has to search for the cause and then work out the solution. There can be many "blind alleys". When the cause of the illness is realised through the heart, the healing can take place almost instantly. On the mental level it is as if the cause is realised, and a forgiveness takes place, and that is the key. The forgiveness is always the key. Forgiveness is the link between mind and heart. The willingness to forgive is the first stage, and happens on a conscious level. The process of forgiving is the connection with the heart which has to happen for the healing to take place. Forgiveness can also take place on the heart level without the awareness of the mind in certain situations. It can happen because of other factors which come together in right timing, as a response to a network of events which impact on the heart in such a way as to instigate a forgiveness. And where there is forgiveness there is always a healing. It may be easier to think of forgiveness as "letting go" of something or someone – of abandoning oneself in a state of trust, or rather, of abandoning the ego, and keeping hold of the truth of the soul.

Where a condition (of the mind) has created illness in the body, the body will heal once the link has been made with soul, and the forgiveness process has happened, but it may then take time for the physical body to repair, even though the healing has taken place, because whereas thought moves instantaneously, physical matter is far more dense and the information must infiltrate from consciousness, and change to physical form. Physical healing can also happen instantly, as we said, if the process happens purely at heart level. Then it seems like a miracle to you, but you must understand that miracles are a natural process, as we said before, where factors come together in right timing to manifest a positive result. It is possible for humans to create miracles, and this is becoming more common. The power of the human mind is beyond anything you can imagine, and as you increase your awareness, and expand your imagination, you will harness more of that power, which is the power to heal. The name of that power is love.

Jesus is recorded as performing many miracles of healing, and we hear of other examples of healings through the ages, usually by people who were later regarded as saints. Are you saying that many ordinary people will have the ability to create miracles of healing?

Yes, many of you already have the ability, and it will become more commonplace.

You say that the human mind is powerful beyond our imagination, but that it is not the mind but the heart which is the centre of healing, and which holds the power to heal?

Do not confuse consciousness with mind. The mind runs on the power, and holds the power to the degree the consciousness will allow, according to the belief of the individual. However, the mind is not the power. The power comes from source.

***

I'm here for a short while.

We are aware that you suffer from muscle fatigue in your back.

Yes! It's been a lot better, but not good today. I think I overdid it with the shopping and housework.

You can heal this completely. Let go.

I'm trying.

Trying is a very negative term to think about. Think only of success. Pour white light into the area – in your imagination – and it will be so. It is healing. Deep-seated anger is causing this and it is time to fully release it. The burning is telling you it is anger. You need to connect with the emotion which has caused the anger. You did that very quickly, which is good because it is the first impression which you must take, without *trying* or thinking or analysing at all. So what is that emotion? Now hold it in your mind. Hold the emotional pain which has caused the anger, and pour white light on it.

What's happening? I have a pain in my chest, and my lower-

34

back/gluteus muscle is pulsing.

That is a sign that the muscles are letting go. Keep pouring the white light on the emotion and the chest area. That represents the heart chakra, where the original pain went in, in vibrational form.

Yes, we know that you have pushed yourself to sit at the computer to write today, but the striving is what you need to let go of, and you must follow your heart. If you do not feel like doing a thing, there is a reason why you should not be doing it. In your case, you needed more rest today. Do not worry! The book will be written. You have had the call to do your creative work. That is the time to drop everything and go to do it. Housework can wait. It is eternal [*laughter*]. Resistance is what is preventing you. It is a habit and it can also be released. It keeps a creative soul chained. Many women have suffered from it. They are afraid of their own power. If they became fully tuned in to their creativity it might create a fire. Their family might rebel. They cannot put themselves before the so-called needs of their children, even though the reality is that their children would love to see them shine, and would benefit from the positive energy which would be released. In your case much fire will be produced when you pick up your brushes again, and that fire will cease to smoulder in your physical body. You are going to need to push through your discomfort to get started. You have been waiting to feel well before starting, but it does not work that way round.

Is this to be included in the book?

Yes. What we are now describing is totally in tune with all which has so far been written. It is because of people not following their hearts that the problems arise. Creative energy repressed is the cause of much disease, because people are not following the contracts they came on Earth to carry out, and their bodies rebel by screaming at them to stop and change what they are doing. Sometimes the creative energy becomes destructive.

***

[*Sometimes the angel voices call unexpectedly.*]

We wish that you type.

I'm here. This is the wrong way round!

We have called you here tonight. Know that all is well and that you are healing your symptoms as you let go of old patterns of thought and belief.

You are a star seed, and this explains many of the physical experiences and symptoms you have suffered as you have transformed yourself. By writing this book you will be leading others forward. By recording your healing, you will show that this is possible in the physical realm. You were called to follow this path, and have come a long way. We mean that you have travelled through eons of time and space to be here. So do not denigrate yourself any longer. You are highly valued as you support many on a spiritual level, which accounts for the exhaustion you experience. We have called you from the washing-up and making of sandwiches, and we are happy that you have heard us.

With respect, dear Angels, the washing-up needs to be done, and the sandwiches made, or we'll be living in chaos, which would be depressing. May I also ask if this is to be left in the book or is for my personal journal?

We laugh. Leave this "interlude" in the book. We understand it is of a personal nature, but we must impress upon you and your readers that though the trappings of your physical life are well and good, and wholesome, at times, the spirit must not be neglected. It is time to shine, and you are procrastinating.

Yes, we know you have had a busy day. We wish you to write a little each day, though. Spirit and body must become as one. Heaven is closer than you think! Heaven moves closer to Earth, and Earth to Heaven. "There shall be a new Heaven and a new Earth", and the time is upon you, and us.

Who are you?

We are angels, and ascended masters, and we are totally for the light, and are from source (from God).

It has gone quiet suddenly. My ears have stopped ringing, I think.

Yes, it is because you have connected with us. Part of the headache problem you suffered was due to the changes taking place, as the new energies bombarded Earth in order to help raise its vibration, and sensitive people were the first to suffer, but many more will be experiencing this as time goes on, and this is why we wish you to record this. Many of your other symptoms, as you have discovered, are undiagnosable, and doctors may use blanket terms such as depression, anxiety, pain and so on to describe them.

Is it okay if we continue this tomorrow?

We thank you for the effort you made tonight.

Thank you. Who was speaking?

Ariel imparts this information to you tonight.

Thank you, Ariel.

***

I'm back, and I'm sorry I didn't wait for you to finish the last communication. I was exhausted and lost the connection with you. I can hardly believe you've just fixed the computer!

You must believe it, dear child! It is imperative that you believe that everything that happens on the Earth plane happens because of thoughts which have manifested reality. Therefore all reality can be changed as thoughts can be changed.

Would an appropriate example be that of my back pain, which returned earlier this evening, causing me to become very fearful that I'd "gone back" to the way I'd been months ago? Somehow I managed to release the pain. Perhaps the glass of wine and chatting to friends on the phone helped me to relax enough to make the change, and what with the computer not working and my asking for your help to fix it, when the computer suddenly went into action, it shocked me out of worrying about my back?

Yes, these are exactly the kinds of events of cause and effect, as they are commonly called, but the reality is that you created the block which stopped the computer, and your change of mind, or should we suggest "change of vibration", created the conditions to set the machine working again. As with your back, the fear made the pain escalate, but the relaxation of wine and so on moved you to a different place from which you felt more powerful. When you asked for help from us, that literally lifted your mind to a higher dimension. We did not fix the computer but enabled you to do it through the power of your mind.

Earlier I visualised myself sitting at the computer writing this dialogue with you. Another part of me was wondering how much it would cost to ask the technician to come out to do the work, but I decided to wait and see if this way would work, and I'm glad that it did (just when I was about to give up, I should add).

That is an important point! It is necessary to give up (control of events) to allow the outcome of your intention to manifest! You have, as we said earlier, a strong will which gets in the way of your manifestations because you are trying to work out how "on Earth" (we laugh) it can come about, and of course this blocks the outcome from manifesting, or holds up the process.

I think you mean that the focus needs to be on the desired result rather than on the process, which is the part we cannot always understand because it is so magic (for want of a better word). And it seems to be outside our earthly experience.

Manifestations use the power which comes from source. You cannot see, feel, touch or understand it because it is a greater power than you are able to even imagine, yet humans have been given the gift to draw on this power to manifest their desires.

This seems more amazing than the magic of fairy stories we read of as children.

Indeed, the stories describe the process of manifestation, disguised as "make believe" within the context of children's stories. How we wish that adults who read these stories to their children would make themselves believe what is right under their noses, as it were.

May I ask, then, if someone is in pain, and trying to manifest good health, or a return to good health, is it the inability to imagine how it feels to be well (because of the hold the pain has on the mind and body) that prevents an instant return to feeling well? If this is the case, doesn't pain get in the way of the healing process?

Yes, it does get in the way, but at the same time the pain is necessary, to let the mind know that the underlying problem is still unsolved. The pain will not return if the problem has been solved. Chronic pain occurs when problems have been only partly dealt with. It is the body's way of drawing attention to itself.

Though I couldn't imagine how the computer could be fixed by prayer, or by directing light, I did find it relatively easy to imagine sitting at the keyboard to write this dialogue this evening. And it has come about. I'm still rather amazed, having fiddled around for nearly three hours trying to sort the problem earlier.

In contrast I don't find it at all easy to imagine myself jumping about pain-free and flexible when I have pain in my back. Do you have any suggestions? I'd like to make the process easier without having to resort to wine.

The pain is a warning from the physical to the mental body to let it know that something is wrong, something which has originated from wrong thinking or wrong action. The physical body will not allow this wrong thinking or action to continue and literally sends out a signal strong enough to attract attention from the mind, even if it means refusing movement. The tendency is to focus on the physical in order to heal the problem, but we are telling you to "go within" to seek the cause of the distress, which originated in the mental/emotional sphere, and heal this. Then the pain will cease and proper movement will resume.

The body is always in the process of repairing and healing, but it is the mind which is sending the pain signal to the area which represents the problem. The healing will be disrupted by further pain if the problem is not addressed at its source. If the body were to heal at this stage, the "lesson" of the problem and its solution would not be learned, and the soul would not progress.

Must we always learn through "pain"? It's a very unpleasant way to have to learn.

Yes, but it is not the "only" way to learn. It is not the best or most natural way. As you know through your teaching, fastest learning takes place through happy and inspiring and joyful experiences.

I'm wondering if creating a happy state of mind could be the key to creating optimum conditions for the body to heal. We hear of people who have laughed themselves back to health. In my experience illness often brings with it a depressed, pessimistic state of mind, and pain certainly does. In these circumstances it seems unnatural to be happy and to laugh.

We say that it can be done, though, and you have achieved this more times than you can know. Laughter and even smiling at a stranger can send powerful healing because it opens the channel for that energy to pass through. It "unblocks".

I've often wondered whether to drive to Edinburgh to go dancing when I've been in pain or mentally low or exhausted. I almost always return home a different person.

We venture to say to you that you *always* return a different person. It is the combination of music and movement which releases and moves the energy. Sometimes the energy is completely transmuted.

If there is tearing in the muscles, though, we do not recommend that you dance, but your body would let you know whether a movement is appropriate or not.

Once you have this knowledge you can artificially induce happiness, and it will heal you. It will manifest into reality. It will become your reality. We rejoice.

What does "rejoice" really mean, dear Angels? You often use the term.

Joy and thanksgiving together lift the worlds to a higher dimension. The physical world, where you abide in your body, connects to the world of your mind and the world of your soul and with Heaven, where God abides, though Heaven is over all. Angels rejoice each and every time a human soul moves to a higher state of consciousness. Angels will also weep when the reverse happens.

If through illness a person were unable to get up and dance, would watching dancing on TV, say, have a beneficial effect?

As long as the person were to visualise himself well and able to dance, and to enter into the spirit of the dancing, then great healing in the muscles would take place.

We would go as far as to say that total healing may take place in certain circumstances.

Miracles may happen, if the person is ready for them, and sometimes even if he is not.

Can you tell me about miracles?

Yes, miracles are the result of instant manifestation, when a decision from the heart is so powerful that the result happens despite the physical conditions. In other words, whatever the physical conditions, an amazing result occurs that would not have seemed possible. All is possible. Miracles happen only in divine right timing and only for the greatest good of all concerned, or the one concerned. Miracles can only be positive.

Thank you, Angels.

Chapter 4

Forgiveness and Trust

Dear Angels,

Can you tell me again about forgiveness, and how a person knows when he has truly forgiven another from the heart?

You speak of your personal issues here, and we are happy to guide you through this. Firstly there must be a desire to forgive, and some of this desire comes from the mind when you realise that holding on to pain is not healthy. The mind then decides it would be a good thing to forgive, but cannot work out how it is done. This is the stage you are at. To truly let go, it is necessary to forgive from the heart. This cannot be done until the time and circumstances are right, for it is not a matter of will. It requires a shift in perspective, and a turn away from the issues which have bound you to the person or situation concerned. It requires you to go outside yourself and to see – no, to *feel* the bigger picture, and to desire to live without the shackles which have bound you into a pattern of resentment and blame. This means taking responsibility for your life as if the person or situation which has harmed you did not exist, accepting the way things are just as they are, and moving forward. Blaming oneself for getting into the situation will not work. That is why it is imperative to forgive oneself.

So how does one forgive oneself, we hear you ask. Go within. Realise that you are forgiven by God, and follow that example. If God sees you as forgiven, why would you go against that? Why would you have a better idea, or better reason, than God? That is why it was said that to enter the kingdom of Heaven it was first necessary to become as a little child. So all you have learned about deserving and rewards for being good will seem defunct, by this simple truth. It is because of fear, and the belief in punishment, that the idea of forgiveness seems so contrary, but if you think about it, it makes complete sense that once an error has been realised, forgiveness is totally appropriate. Errors are to help you learn. Once learned, simply let go and try another way. With a continual focus on the light, and a loving heart, it becomes much more rare to make mistakes which cause a person to become bound to another, and to build resentment. The heart will be the test of truth, in any given situation. If it does not *feel* right, do not do it; if it does, do it!

Thank you, Angels. I'll be back later to ask how you can tell whether a response is from the heart or from the mind.

We are happy to communicate on this.

***

[*The angels asked me to transfer the following communication from my personal journal to this document, and I now realise that it also answers my last question about discerning between heart and mind responses.*]

We open the door for you. It is the door of forgiveness and cannot be entered except by way of the heart. Love, light, health and happiness lie on the other side and can be accessed once you have passed through. You will know when this has happened because you will feel different. And your life will change for the better.

The world is beautiful, but it is only a picture, an illusion, and another world lies beyond. This other world can be accessed by the human mind that is connected to a loving heart. Love is the key; forgiveness is the door which connects the two worlds. It is necessary to practise moving from one to the other and living in the spiritual world with your material existence based in the physical world. (This will be made easier.)

The power to forgive comes from the heart. It should feel large but light, not heavy and cold. You may feel tears – tears of relief, not sadness. You will feel lighter in your body. And more secure. You will feel healthier and more powerful. And calm.

When you think of the person concerned you will not feel any confusing emotions arising from your belly. Saying, "I forgive X from the heart" will help. Even if the process is not complete, it has to reach its conclusion once started. You cannot go back. This is where the willingness of the mind comes into play, though. It is important to understand that it is from the heart that the forgiveness takes place. We stress that you do not need to feel love or respect for the person or to condone his actions. You are simply letting go.

A suitable visualisation might be to see it as dirty water and gunge sucked down the drain, but with the people concerned staying intact. Then you can love them in the wider sense of the meaning – that is, unconditionally. You will definitely know when the process is complete.

Release the past and move forward now. Forgive all who have held you back. Forgive yourself. This is our final answer to all ills – it is the way out.

White candles are necessary for the forgiving. One for each person you focus on. Write down the words and let them burn out. Let each person go. Be at peace now.

***

What do you wish me to write?

Direct light around yourself as much as possible and tell your friends to do this also – by "friends" we mean those whom you know to be on this path, and those who are awake and aware.

If you surround yourself with light, then you are protected and we can reach you far more easily, and impart the necessary information to each one of you, for it is at this time that Heaven awaits those who are able and willing to seek the truth. They shall be given the ability to manifest their gifts in this world, and their abilities will become tenfold if they work with the light. For all negativity will fall away, and that energy which bound itself and the person concerned to darkness will emerge as positive and work towards the healing of the world. Faith is necessary, and we stress that time is short, and it will require a leap of faith for many to do this.

We believe it possible, though. We remind you that the transformation always takes place from the heart, and there may be no outward sign of change except that the person concerned will feel differently.

Forgiveness is a necessary step, as is patience (which is your new challenge), and overall there is a need for trust.

These are all difficult areas for those who have dwelt in fear, but it is necessary to understand that fear is illusion, and can be cast out, and when that happens love will abound.

Love is the key, and many hold the key, not knowing that it is connected with a door. That is the door we call "forgiveness". It is only possible to find the door if the key is held by those of a pure heart, who are able to love unconditionally all things of the world. Love will draw them to the door and trust is the drive which will push them through, and once through they are in the light and have come home. They can then truly work for the light and for the glory of God.

Can you tell me about trust?

Trust is not acquired with experience; rather it tends to be lost with experience, especially if the experience has been somewhat negative. Though the experience, whether positive or negative, has been of great value in the teaching of life lessons, the trust is often a casualty on that very path which draws a person to wisdom in this life. Trust was there with the newborn child, with the soul which came to this earth, but was lost again, as the child gained its personality.

Faith is necessary to believing that trust is intact, and like an archaeologist with faith as his spade, a person must carefully dig deep to find his trust again under so much rubble of the ages. It can be found by asking –

[*At this point the angels' answer broke off. It was completed in a much later communication, during which I was told that earlier messages on trust had been unfinished because I hadn't been ready to receive them, not being trusting enough at the time to take the words down. The finished message appears at the beginning of Chapter 11, the chapter specifically on trust. (The angels are making a joke as I write this: they are instructing me – with much laughter – to tell the reader not to flick to the end of the book now to get the answer!)*]

***

Is my friend's interpretation of the faith/trust meaning sound – that of "savoir" and "pouvoir", the "savoir" being faith and the "pouvoir" being trust? In other words, faith is the belief and trust is the acting on that belief? It's necessary to have the faith but the test lies in acting upon the faith, which is the trust?

It is similar to the forgiveness process in that there must first be willingness of the mind, and the action arises from the condition of the heart. We speak often about the heart and that is because this is the chakra which connects a person to love in its many aspects, and in particular to divine love. Through this connection, a soul can access its salvation, and even change its karma. Love is the ingredient which can transcend any situation and change it. Love transforms. This is a universal truth. All humans are capable of experiencing love, but it is a choice.

***

Are you there?

We are here. We are guiding you. All is well.

We remind you to visualise light within and around yourself. Send it outwards to people and situations. Then we can more easily connect. We ask you to practise sending white light outwards. We are here to help, and you can ask us anything you desire. We see you and can reach you when you work with the light. Doors are opening for those who desire to follow God's will. We hear your call and are by your side always. Trust us. We desire you speak with us. Salvation happens one soul at a time.

Work on the trust. Many understand our messages, and the universal laws in principle. There are many books to explain it. However, you cannot live in the light until you live by these laws and practise them daily. This requires a shift in consciousness. It requires trust. We invite you to step over the boundaries which hold you back, and into the light, where love and happiness, beauty and plenitude, abound. We constantly remind you of this world beyond, which can be lived in simultaneously.

***

Are you here?

We are with you always.

I think I was expecting to feel good because we'd connected, then was shocked at feeling a bit down and lethargic, and at finding it hard to get on with the everyday things or be inspired to move forward with other things.

We understand you, and it is because you are not yet putting your faith into practice (which is the trust) that you need to keep working on it, and we can promise that it will become easier. The fear is a block of old negative emotions. It needs to be cast out. Then you will feel differently. It is indeed the hardest part, at whatever level the fear has manifested. Throw light at it and it has to dispel. Keep going. It requires patience with self to push through, but we are behind you and will not let you fall. We urge you to move on, and you will reach the place of light even though you still doubt, because you cannot feel the peace of mind yet, but it is to come.

All you are conveying to me makes sense, and is in keeping with other sources I'm reading. But I'm still experiencing resistance, sadness, frustration, as well as neck pain, some fear, impatience with myself, and worry that I'm not up to it. I still feel I'm very ego-based as a person, and very much in need of love and approval. So it seems as if I'm getting too far ahead of myself in writing all of this.

We tell you again that you have the power to move through all of this, and to heal yourself, and we are helping you. Let go of ego-based thoughts and allow the help to come in. Love is the only real power there is, so thinking that you can control events from the thinking of your mind is a false belief. Let this go.

I fear letting it go in case I get lost in the process.

That is the fear of ego at work, and you know that you are more than that.

I don't feel I have the strength.

The strength comes from the heart. Work from the heart.

How do you find the way to happiness?

Our answer to you is always the same: go through the forgiveness, and then you will come to find light and happiness – and love. Where love is, fear cannot exist. Love dispels fear. Clearing out negativity by forgiving will bring a soul to love.

***

Are you there?

It is time – it is time. We guide you in this communication, to take down our instruction, so it may be clearer to you, and to those who may read these words. All must be healed. We are calling many of you to follow the path of light. It is now possible on Earth to find hope and salvation. Open your hearts to love. The love will heal and transform you. Forgiveness is the way. Any bad feelings harboured in the heart will impede progress, and create problems which will manifest in the physical body. There is now no time to work through the longer-term effects of these illnesses. It is necessary to heal the current situations and not to manifest more for the future. The world can no longer support fear-based entities, and its energy is needed to heal itself, and even then much help is needed from those who work with Earth energies.

You have spoken of the need for forgiveness, and given instruction on how to achieve this, and of the need for trust, and of the transforming power of love. Are there other qualities necessary?

Yes – gratitude is one such quality. It is a gateway, and provides a connection between the physical and divine realms. The gratitude needs to be heartfelt, not imposed by the will out of duty.

What's the difference between gratitude and prayer?

True gratitude is one form of prayer – in fact, one of its purest forms, which carries much positive energy towards its focus.

All reactions which come from a loving heart will help move the Earth back into line with its natural self-healing ability. By this we mean that the thoughts and actions of mankind that come from a loving heart have a positive effect on the physical environment.

From this I understand that the physical environment can even benefit instantly from a positive thought towards it from one person. The long-term effects of enough people thinking such thoughts would cause others to stop physical destruction, such as adding pollutants to the soil.

Do not underestimate the power of the thoughts of one person.

We tell you to follow your hearts, because that which comes from the heart comes from God and increases the light in the world. Many are affected by the actions of those who work from the heart, and the blessings are multiplied. Those of you who have gifts, talents and abilities know that it takes faith to follow the call, and to practise and work. Yet the work is a joy, and is what you love doing, and the result of the creation brings pleasure and joy to many. It increases well-being in those who receive, and enables them to open their hearts in turn, and pass something on in turn. Love thrives on the joy which is thus created and expands itself. Fear cannot exist where love is, and love heals. Love is the light which dispels the darkness.

So what we are saying to you is that using your gifts is a very good way to help heal yourselves, others and the Earth. The ripples will go out, and never cease.

Love is the only real power there is. We accelerate this power here in the angelic realms, but we are reliant on humans being willing to help raise the vibration of the Earth with pure intentions coming from the heart. These are then manifest, and the acceleration of the love vibration takes place.

Your love for each other, for animals, plants and the natural world, helps the healing process. We hear your thoughts of gratitude for the beauty of the Earth, and we intercede in the Earth's healing. (From Ariel.)

**

I'm here to take down your words.

Trust us. Trust us when we tell you about the power of love and the miraculous healing which can occur because of it.

Well, my headache of the past two and a half years has miraculously disappeared, but I now have backache and can hardly sit at the computer to type. I fear it will be a long process to heal it, and am exhausted by having had constant pain for all this time. Can you advise me?

Child, you know that you have created this, and that forgiveness is the necessary step you must take to heal it. You must forgive from the heart all who have held you back, including yourself.

Yes, you've often told me this, and I've been unsure whether it was a matter for my personal journal or one to write about here, but I decided to write about it here as it relates directly to other issues you speak of. I hope someone reading this might be helped by it. I feel as if I'm having to work through all of these questions – forgiveness, trust, patience, fear, depression, pain and so on – even as I'm writing your book! Is it appropriate to write about my personal issues here?

Yes, it is why you have been chosen for this task. You are learning to work from the heart (which is sometimes difficult for you as you have such a strong will – and this is, by the way, partly why you suffered the head pain for so long, because of the conflict of pathways between heart and mind). You have begun to trust again, and now you are dealing with the remnants of fear held in the body, which over time creates pain, and this is why it is in your back; in fact, you are sitting on it. It is old pain from the past and you must let it go. This means forgiving the appropriate people. Then it will go.

I've been working on forgiveness for ages, but I still have a long way to go.

You have wanted to forgive and thought about it very much, but that is not the same as doing it. It must be done from the heart, not the mind.

Yesterday I thought I experienced a "letting go", though I don't know how it happened or why it happened then.

We can answer that for you. You had given up hope of an outcome, and let yourself go. You accepted what was happening without a need to control the outcome. That is what creates the transformation.

I also asked for your help.

Yes. We desire that you ask for help on all issues, great or small, but it is *you* who have to do the "letting go" where an issue such as forgiveness is concerned.

When I go away from writing this, it's my intention to do some forgiving from the heart as you described earlier in the book, and I'll then report on the outcome.

We happily await the result, and do not forget to call on us for help. You are feeling resistance to doing this?

Yes, and I don't know why.

In some cases it is easier to stay stuck in the pain and benefit from being a person who has an excuse not to live to his full potential.

Is this true in my case? I feel that I'm always wishing I were free to live to my full potential!

Yes, on one level. On the conscious level of your mind you are absolutely desperate to have the health you need to live your life to the full, but on some other levels you have been blocked. Some of this is not your fault and some is of your own making, out of fear or beliefs which are limiting. Now you have the capacity to throw out all of this and live from the heart the way you have wished to with your mind. We know it is not easy – to throw out fear, for instance – but as we always say to you, it can be done, and you have come a long way. Anyone can do it.

We have heard your questions. First we must say this. If and when you fully forgive yourself, then you open the door for miracles in your life. These may be to do with complete healing, with your occupation, with your relationships, happiness and so forth.

It is necessary to let go completely, and allow the light of God to envelop your soul. Then all false thinking falls away, and the ego has no more need to prove your worth, as you know that you are already of the greatest worth. You know this from the heart. Then there is no more room to take on the burdens of guilt, shame or unworthiness. And you do not carry others' burdens either, because you understand that it is their responsibility to follow their own true path, as it is yours to follow your own.

At this point you will find that you are connecting with all who are realising this simple truth. You will be souls on the same path.

So, we tell you to pray for one another. Release your burdens, for there is no need to carry these weights. Ask for your desires to be met, and in truth they will be met. Ask from the heart. The heart can only ask for that which it truly needs. Know that your needs are met, when you ask. And act on your intuition, which comes from the heart. This will speed the process.

Thank you, Angels.

Chapter 5

The Transforming Power of Light

Dear Angels,

I don't know what to ask. I think I'm here just to see if any ideas come to me, or if you have any message for me.

The veil is thinning – the veil between Heaven and Earth. Those who are awake and aware see the beauty of creation and sense the love in all situations, good and bad. But those who are not aware are resisting allowing the light to come in. It is too bright for them to discern, and they fight against it in earnest, and take drastic measures to hold on to their false beliefs. The darkness will increase in the world for a time because of the actions of those whose existence is fear-based. They have built their lives around false beliefs, and know no other way. Some will experience a conversion, and come to the light. Yet more will cease to exist on the Earth plane. Light dispels the dark, which is why we ask many of you to hold the light, for yourselves and for others to see by. We connect with your light and guide you forward. We weep for the devastation that man has created, and the acts of inhumanity that man has committed, but we rejoice that salvation is possible.

***

We see you. We ask that you type. You are to help others by increasing your light, and by connecting with them through focusing on the heart energy.

I tried to do that at the station the other night, and the belligerent-looking man to whom I'd offered a seat immediately moved away, apologising that he didn't want to smoke near me. Is this the kind of thing you mean?

Precisely that. You do not even need to speak or to understand how the light works. You just need to keep using it. This will create more energy and light for further use. You can have fun with it, but keep your intention pure, and concentrate on the highest good manifesting for all concerned (as you learned through Louise Hay).

How do you focus on heart energy?

If you have a pure intention and visualise light (pure white is good for general purpose), then that is enough to establish the heart connection.

How do I increase my light?

Just imagine.

Do you need to keep concentrating on the light for ages, or can you send one quick blast, and leave it at that (if you're in a hurry, or talking to someone, for instance)?

We laugh at your terminology.

A "quick blast" is okay, but we prefer a more sustained effort if possible. You can ask that the energy continues to flow once you have stopped consciously sending it, though, and then move on to send it out again in your next situation.

I think it will take some discipline to keep this going.

It is easier and more fun than worrying all the time – which by the way sends out a lot of negative energy to the situation concerned, and is ultimately counter-productive. You have no idea of the power of your mind.

Point taken. It takes an effort to change the beliefs and habits of a lifetime, though.

We say to you that these can be changed instantly if you so wish, and that this could create miracles. On a more serious note, the resistance you experience is created by the turning away from your old patterns. If you imagine a physical body which has gained momentum in one direction (such as a boat) trying to do a U-turn, you will understand why there is turbulence, and the denser the energy, the harder it is to turn.

Do you mean that the darker the soul's path, the harder it is to change.

Yes. It can be done, though, and if light is sent to the situation by others, then that will greatly ease the situation. That is why Jesus said to pray for all who persecute you. That is why it makes sense to pray for or send light to world leaders and all who can influence or change the path of destruction.

Is sending out light the same as prayer?

Prayer is more specific, and people will do it when there is a deep need, and they or their loved ones need help. Sending light is more general, and has the benefit that it will go where it is most needed. It is also more appealing to those who do not hold any particular faith or belong to any particular denomination. You do not need to have any idea where the light is going, but believe us when we tell you that it does reach its destination. It is as real as you are.

We angels will help you. When you see how we operate in your life, your faith in us will increase, and we can help you more, and help you to enjoy your life, and reach your full potential.

***

Do you have any communication for me?

We wish that you type. We need you for the light. It is all in right timing that we connect with you. The world is at crisis point in its evolution, and the forces of darkness are gathering in opposition to the increasing light. It is important, as we have told you, not to fear, and to keep the light flowing around you and out into the world. You are protected and the light you send cannot be used for any other purpose than for healing, and to help the Earth raise its vibration. This can be done. Do not buy into others' fear, or the fear generated by reports of evil in the media. Send light, but do not dwell on the horror, as this only feeds the darkness. By sending the light you can help a situation in ways that you could hardly believe possible. Those who are dying have elected to do so in this life. It is all part of the greater plan. We are here to help all those of you who remain on Earth – to guide you through the necessary transformation, which is going to happen now. It has to happen for Earth's survival and entry to the higher realms in terms of its vibration.

Who speaks to me?

Uriel speaks, and Amber is here. Jacob is directing us.

Who is Jacob?

Archangel Sandalphon works with him at this time.

Have I taken this down correctly?

Trust us. We are here and are guiding you. We rejoice for the love that is created by those of you who are able to manifest and increase the light. Many shall be healed. The Earth itself shall be healed and its vibration lifted to connect with the higher realms. All is well.

Many changes are taking place in your world, and people are feeling this. You do not have to be a "sensitive" to know this. Many are feeling confused. Those of you who are awake and aware need to stand firm in order to help those who do not know what is happening. You must also monitor your thoughts, so as to make sure you are consistently standing in the light and attracting positive experiences to you. You begin to realise that you are manifesting experiences very quickly, so it is important to keep track of your mind and seek the joy and happiness in life *no matter what* is happening around you and to other people. Do not fear if you hear bad news, but focus on the light to help bring about positive change. This is not always easy for you but we will help, and it is okay to consistently ask for help on all issues, and to tell your friends to do this also. Send out the white light, as we have told you, to help heal the world and yourself. Direct it outwards to the world and inwards for yourself. Play with it, as a boy would play with a football. The light can go anywhere and help any situation to which it is directed.

It is time to resolve all issues in your life, to forgive all who have hurt you, as we have described, and to follow your path (unimpeded), for this is the purpose which brought you to Earth, and much good will come from your actions if you truly follow your heart. Blessed are those who are willing to seek the light and the love which is within every situation.

We must repeat what we have said about the power of the human mind, and the power of the light which can be sent by the will of your mind and from the desire of your heart. This light can reach any and all situations and create a positive effect. It can arrive instantly at any point on the globe – anywhere you wish. You do not need to know or understand how the light works, as long as you hold the intention for it to reach its destination. We cannot help unless you ask us, and then we can also work with the light that you have created. We repeat that you have no idea of the power of your mind. You must believe us and trust, and work with the light in all situations. When this light is sent, it cannot be interrupted or used for any other purpose than the intention of the person who has sent it. It cannot be extinguished or diminished.

You must know that darkness is absence of light, and that fear is absence of love, and that worry is absence of trust, and therefore that darkness, fear and worry are not powers in themselves, but carry a negative vibration which is contrary to their opposites. This negative vibration can only be extinguished by overwhelming them with the opposite energy – thus trust will overcome worry, and so on.

This opposite energy is a higher, faster vibrational energy, and is therefore stronger, and can therefore win out over its denser form, which is its opposite.

Worrying about worry, fearing fear and exploring darkness only adds to and augments those things.

What is an enlightened person?

Quite literally it is one who has come into the light because he has dispelled the darkness. He has come through the darkness and into the light, and he has much light around him, and this affects all who come into contact with him. He has made the choice himself to turn away from sin (which is the path of darkness) and into light. He has made his own light, and this has connected him with light from the highest source, which is God. This may have been a process which took place over many lifetimes, so that in each life he entered he was more enlightened. It is not an immediate process, because it is necessary to learn through being in the dark, in different lives. But the light which has been created in each life can be carried to the next, and built upon. Truly, there are so many of you whose light is so bright that we see you shine. You will have noticed that there is much wisdom in your languages, and much truth in commonplace phrases such as "being in the dark", or "shining faces", or "coming from the heart", and there are so many more. People often do not realise that these expressions are real (not metaphors), and that they can be realised by the power of the mind.

I found the word "enhalo" in the dictionary just now as I was looking for something else.

We found it for you and you can practise putting light around yourself. We can see the light of people who are deliberately imagining it around them. Their imaginings become real. Such is the power of the human mind.

If our commonplace expressions are so full of these descriptions of spiritual states, then why are we still "in the dark" as a human race? Why do we think that they are just metaphors, and not believe that someone, somewhere, knew them to be real? We see and feel these effects, as we see a person's face which shines, or feel the darkness. Yet we still do not believe that it is a spiritual thing.

I keep being reminded of the early Quakers, who called themselves "children of the light" and spoke of "walking in the light", or "holding a person in the light", and of how George Fox overcame the "ocean of darkness" and found the "ocean of light above the ocean of darkness", and how he preached that Christ Jesus had come to teach the people Himself, and that they had to experience the teachings for themselves rather than through a minister.

The early Quakers were "right on (target)", as you would say. You yourself experienced a conversion to the truth in 1985 at the World Gathering of Young Friends.

Yes, I remember so vividly talking to John on the bus, and suddenly everything made sense and was so clear, but not long afterwards the experience faded.

You had an "opening" there, but the time was not right and you were too easily influenced by those who saw John as a "religious nut" (as you would say), whereas he was the opposite. This is where fear comes in and stops a person from seeing beyond the veil, even though he has glimpses of the reality beyond. He cannot take it in. You can understand now that you felt the truth of it all in your heart, but did not believe your heart. You had more to learn. You can see how even the simple message of George Fox has been misunderstood by the very people who promote his message. And it is nearly the same story in most religions and faiths of the world. The truth is too simple to see.

Believe us when we say that the light is real, and the darkness is created by fear, and can be cast out or dispelled by the light.

Why is it necessary to go through the darkness at all to get to the light?

Now you are asking!

God made the Earth, and human life on Earth, to see what would happen if souls had a choice. It was necessary for a soul to have a physical experience, in order to have the chance to manifest its choice in the physical.

Do you mean that we didn't need to go down the path of fear? And if we hadn't, then would we have had anything to learn at all? Would we have gone straight to light and been bodiless?

You would have had a very different experience of the physical world, and beautiful experiences. This is still to come – at the eleventh hour. It is all in right timing.

Are you truly saying that we are a kind of divine experiment?

Yes. But you had the choice to be in it and the chance of experiencing Heaven on Earth, and it is to pass, and we greatly rejoice.

Thank you, Angels.

Chapter 6

Letting Fear Go

Dear Angels,

I haven't written for some time. I don't know where to begin.

We are helping you. We are guiding you in this process of learning to trust again. You know when you are, and when you are not, as the energy feels different. Learn to be able to distinguish the difference between these feelings, and then it will be your aim to trust continually, and you can then walk the path of light without fear. Fear is always the block which prevents a person from staying in the light, and which causes him to relegate experiences of being in the light to being the exception rather than the rule within his everyday life. We are telling you to make it your personal rule to keep continually in the light. Miracles will then routinely manifest in your life, and your energy will focus on moving smoothly and joyously on your life path. We emphasise the joy.

All pain and difficulty, whether physical or emotional, is created, as you know from your life experience, when a soul becomes "off centre". It can take a person a lifetime or many lifetimes to correct his path towards healing and wholeness, but we are telling you that it is now imperative for those of you who will live to see the dawn of the new age to correct your path now, and to heal yourselves. This is why there are so many of us waiting to help in all areas of your lives, and with issues both great and small. All must be resolved and healed.

You can now sense joy and gratitude welling up within you for no apparent reason. It is not that you did not experience these feelings before, but you needed good reasons and good experiences to allow them to surface, but these feelings are a natural part of you. Laura, you have often – almost always – felt these intense feelings of gratitude and joy when in the wilds of nature, because you are deeply attuned to the vibration of nature, which is wholesome and uncorrupted and is itself connected with the divine. You have sensed this. Now you can establish these feelings as the normal base from which you act out your life. Fear is not a natural part of you. It is a reaction which enables you to get quickly out of physical danger. It serves no useful purpose within the emotional body, but destroys a soul and turns it to darkness. It is used by those who are themselves trapped in fear, and corrupted, to pull others down with them, either on an individual basis or on a massive scale – for example, in situations of conflict and war. A government can terrorise its people with fear. Fear becomes, in the imagination, worse than pain. Fear is illusion, but is made real by the imagination, and then creates havoc – from causing illness in an individual mind or body to destruction and death on a larger scale. Fear tactics are and will be used against those who are seeking the light and a peaceful means to resolve conflict. Fear can be overcome on an individual basis, and if enough people work together to dispel fear, then fear can have no hold over them collectively.

Fear, fear, fear. Fear is at the root of all evil. Mankind has habitually turned from the truth because of it. In the past, many enlightened ones were finally put to death because they would have been too powerful against the forces of the dark. But they have carried their truth forever onwards. There are more enlightened souls who walk the Earth now than ever before, and their light has created a fire so bright that the forces of darkness can be challenged. If enough of you turn to the light, and away from darkness – and time is short – the world can be saved. By that we mean that God will keep his creation, and love will reign supreme. Fear itself will be driven out. We know that you can hardly imagine this, but it is now the only way the Earth can survive. The Earth itself has raised its vibration and cannot support the darker forces. Too much light, too high a vibration, cannot nurture fear-based entities.

It is not only humans that evolve, but the animal, mineral and plant kingdoms evolve too.

***

It's late, but I've a feeling that you're here and may wish to speak?

Be reassured that we will be here and guiding you to take down our communication. Do not weep, dear child, for you are loved by so many in the physical and the higher realms. We will guide you through your pain, and you will be healed and happy again. It is all in right timing.

I weep sometimes when I can feel your presences with me, and it makes me feel my humanity all the more keenly.

You still have no idea of the power of the human mind that can connect with spirit, and soar into the higher realms. Be comforted that you are on this path and are stepping over this invisible boundary into the light.

Thank you, Angels. Who was speaking?

Sandalphon.

***

I'm here. Are you there?

We are here and we guide you to take down our words.

We must continue on the subject of fear. We insist that fear must be eradicated as the motivating force behind both personal and global issues. Fear is created by the human mind, and is the cause of most pain and destruction. This cannot continue. The world is healing fast but much fear rises to the surface as the healing takes place. New wars are taking place and people must now make choices about their future – not just politicians, but all who are able to make a choice must decide on what they believe, and act on it. There is no time for "sitting on the fence". People must be brought to the realisation that they can use the power of their minds to create their destiny, individually and collectively. When enough people are acting on their beliefs, and when their beliefs originate from the heart, then change will happen fast. Healing will happen.

What happens if people are acting in all sincerity on beliefs which are profound but misled? What happens when their beliefs come not from the heart but from the mind – from indoctrination or ignorance?

Everyone has a heart, and the heart is the test of truth. Everyone has the ability to sense whether he is acting from heart or from mind. He is not acting with sincerity if he is acting from a mind which is indoctrinated, or blinded by ignorance.

If a person has suffered – for instance, a child growing up in a war-torn country, living with injustice, seeing abuses of human rights within his family, suffering pain, both physical and emotional, and hunger – then it wouldn't be surprising, would it, if that person became indoctrinated, or grew up to be a persecutor himself? We see it happen all the time.

This is true. But unless a person becomes so damaged that he is affected mentally, he can still have the inner knowing of what is true and good, and of what is cruel and destructive. The human body–mind system is always growing towards enlightenment –

searching for the truth, realising goodness, beauty, joy, kindness, compassion and gratitude, and the reward is in health and happiness, success, and further joy. The motivation is always towards the light. Fear creates suffering and blocks a person from achieving his true destiny. The perpetrators of fear, who are aware of their evil-doing, are furthest from the light, and in most need of help.

We ask all those of you who are awake and aware to consistently send the light out to places and people who are living in fear and darkness because of the patterns which have been generated by fear itself. All must be healed and miracles can and do happen, and those who are the worst perpetrators of fear can turn to the light and work powerfully for the light and for the glory of God.

We cannot help them change without those of you on Earth who are willing to send your light, which then creates bridges for us to cross. Then we can assist the healing of mankind. No one has the power to force change when acting from the truth of his heart. It is by the example of those who are acting from the truth of their hearts that the hearts and minds of those who are witness to their acts are changed. Everyone is given opportunities to change. Everyone – not a select few. It is a choice. You have free will to make a choice from the heart, even if the outcome does not seem possible in the physical world. Making the decision from the heart will create the conditions which bring about the change in the physical world. Making the decision from the heart, and acting upon it, even without any hope or evidence of the possibility of seeing a change take place in the physical world – that is the trust. Trust is necessary. This will bring about the change.

***

I'm here to continue your book. I wish to continue. I've been reading over what you've said so far, and it makes far more sense to me than it did before. I know that it represents universal truth. My difficulty now is in accepting that this information has been given to me, as it is beyond the scope of my mind.

Dear child, it may be beyond the scope of your conscious mind at present, but it is not beyond the scope of your unconscious mind, which has the ability to reach far out beyond your universe, beyond known places and times, beyond the future and the past. You have no idea of the power of your mind, and what filters from your unconscious mind to the conscious aspect of yourself will become your future reality. So this means that you are evolving with your mind. You seek the truth, you are given answers to your questions, and you come to accept these answers. You begin to live the reality created by your mind, rather than living the illusion created by fear.

I still carry a lot of fear regarding my health and my financial situation.

However, you are beginning to understand the connection between thought and creation, and how it is your thoughts that create your every experience in life, including your health and your financial situation. You have conquered much of your ill health and the pains in your body, and we applaud you for your faith in the process of ridding fear from this aspect of your psyche or consciousness. Your improved health will give you the incentive to conquer the other problems you see as being part of your life.

Is the shoulder pain part of this process?

We laugh. It is so obvious, is it not, that pains carried in the shoulder represent what you are carrying – what you are bearing?
We tell you that you need bear nothing. It is your attitude

which creates the pain.

Do you mean that if I bear my responsibilities with courage, happiness and joy, then they cease to be burdens?

Yes. You have learned this.

But I still have the pain. I thought I'd got rid of it earlier this year, but it came back.

That is because you went back to a former mindset. You knew how to heal it, but you did not act on your intuition, but went back to a former thought pattern, which brought back the pain. You must remember exactly what you were doing when you first noticed the pain return.

I was on the phone listening to a friend relate her problems to me.

Words well chosen! You have said yourself that there was a relation between you and the problems of your friend. You took on her load just by listening. You allowed her burden to add to your own. It was too much for your shoulder to bear. This is a habit and you must stop it.

I thought I'd brought on the problem purely by bad posture, by tensing unconsciously and creating blockage in an area which had not fully recovered from the last problem.

We laugh at the words you have unconsciously chosen to so accurately describe the process! Now you must consciously choose words which will train your thoughts along a different route and eliminate the pain for good. We are giving you a hint.

So I take this to mean that I need to make a positive affirmation, because less than positive ways of thinking and speaking build up patterns which ultimately create physical conditions of illness and pain. I might say something like "My shoulder is now totally comfortable as I joyfully accept my own responsibilities." That sounds ridiculous.

It is a pity you think this ridiculous, and you would not have the pain if you did not.

We have spoken before of following your heart in all things and following your own truth in all situations – your own truth and not someone else's.

This partly means taking your own responsibility and not someone else's. That is for that person to deal with.

Do you understand us?

Yes, I think you are telling me that on some level I took on my friend's burden because I thought it was what I ought to be doing as a friend.

Again we laugh at your choice of words. "Ought" and "should(er)" are the very words which create the *atmosphere*, the *mindset*, the *conditions*, for that tension in the body to grow. It is a direct reflection of your thoughts. In this case there is a direct connection between your shoulder pain and thoughts that you should and ought to do or be things which run contrary to your natural state. It is because you believe you have to justify your existence on some level, to pay back to life by taking things on, whereas the real truth is that all that you have and all that you are is given and accepted. Anything you cannot accept manifests as illness or problem in some outer form. The shoulder is where burdens are carried. It must become your responsibility to rid as much as you can of any weight which impedes your progress. Go lightly. It is all illusion anyway. Nothing matters so much that you have to carry it all on your own shoulder.

With respect, dear Angels, you keep using the word "must". Is this not the same as "should" or "ought"?

We qualify what we say by adding that if you desire to heal your pain there is no other way than to change consciously or unconsciously. This is why we use the word "must". But make it easy and pleasant for yourself. Do not turn our word, "must", into a burden on yourself. We do not criticise. We do not attempt to "improve" you. You are already perfect and have within you the skills to "drop" that which impedes your happiness and progress.

It is all fear. It is all about learning to release the fear to uncover the true joy which life has to offer. It was never meant to be a struggle!

So why is it that some people can trust more easily, believe without seeing and so on, and others find it more difficult?

Again we say, it is a matter of choice. Choose not to believe, and you will not see.

What makes us choose or not choose to believe, then?

This is complex, yet simple.

As you know, I have difficulty with trusting. I think I'm better at having faith than trust. To take myself as an example – what would you say to me? Is there anything I can do to trust more? Earlier you said that it's all a matter of choice, but I don't feel I have a choice as to whether I'm trusting or not.

Our answer to you is always the same. You must go through the blocks which stop you from moving forward. You must move through the pain, if there is pain, through the fear, if there is fear. Your problem arises because of fear of what might happen if you were to trust completely – fears such as "What will happen to me?" "What will people think of me?" "What if this or that horrible scenario were to happen?" "If I *let go* and trust, will some change take place to make this or that happen?" And you fear the worst, because you understand from your past that certain undesirable things can happen. But we want you to know and to believe that it is because of your thought waves, which are untrusting, that you can attract to you such undesirable outcomes.

When you look at the bigger picture, you can see that everything has worked out ultimately, despite the glitches. When you trust that all is well, then you cannot make things worse by your trusting. Only better.

It is fear that is the block, because of past events, or awareness of past events. You see how a baby is fearless. Through programming, the fear begins to take hold. The trust becomes a casualty.

We said earlier that it is necessary to dig as an archaeologist digs through the layers of earth to find the treasure. The trust is there, but it may be buried. We tell you to cast out your fear, and the trust you will find. Seek and ye shall find, knock and the door is opened.

Work on the trust.

Can I return to what you said earlier about it being a matter of choice?

Yes, the choice is in the turning to light, in the decision to forgive all, to find the trust, buried beneath the faith. The choice is in the turning to light.

The road will become easier. It is the casting out of fear that is the hardest part, but it can be done, if you constantly ask for help, and for light to guide you. The light is always there. It is only "hidden" by fear. Fear casts its shadow. It is only a shadow. It is illusion. The light is real and can never be extinguished. Throw light at the fear, and the fear cannot remain. Where there is light, there cannot be darkness in the same place. Where there is worry, there cannot be trust. Choose to cast away the fear, the worry. By that action, you are trusting.

Practise! And do not berate yourself for anything, for you are perfect in our eyes!

Words can't express my gratitude that I don't have to be punished, or to punish myself, any longer. Words can't express my relief as I come to the understanding that there was never any need for the struggle I've been in, and the pain I've been in, which I realise has been self-inflicted.

Child, do not be so harsh with yourself. You did not have enough pieces of the picture of life to see the overall pattern, as it were. You were raised in a climate of fear, and had to seek the love for yourself. You had to seek the love that life had to offer in the harsh lessons you learned. To that extent, you fulfilled your role on Earth, with the greatest of courage and faith. We applaud you for your commitment to the joy, albeit that you have received much pain. We promise you that this is now to end, and that life will become one joy for you.

You are forgiven. This is your reward. Heaven can be found on Earth. Heaven is here, and there. It exists outwith the mind of man. It exists within the reach of the heart of man. It exists above all in the realms which are surrounding the Earth at this time.

You do not understand this yet, but you shall, in time.

The Earth is in crisis, but is healing, and Heaven is connecting with Earth, in a way that has never before been witnessed by man.

You are sensitive. You understand this, even without any knowledge or explanation.

It is through the heart of man – we speak collectively – it is through those children of faith who have the ability to stretch out their hearts to meet us and take down our words – and you are one – that *the earth is saved.*

Thank you, Angels.

Chapter 7

Sources of Evil

Dear Angels,

What about evil? Is that a power?

Evil is not in itself a power but it uses and runs on power which has been corrupted. It takes away the energy from the true power as a parasite weakens its host. Fear is opposite love. Evil is the effect of that process of corruption.

What is it that causes the corruption? What is the drive that drives the evil? If love comes from God or "source", where does evil come from?

Evil is as evil does. Evil exists only as manifestation. It is not part of the divine plan. It is a corruption. You are asking who wills evil into existence. It was brought forth on Earth by man. That is the story of man's "fall" from grace. There are many versions of the story, but we tell you that it is happening continually.

Am I understanding this correctly? Evil is not part of God's creation but has manifested as a corruption of some other power. If not God's intention, then how can it exist and persist?

God allowed for Earth to evolve, for the programme to run, as we said before, to see what would happen. Man was allowed free will. As you know, the entire planet is now under threat of self-destruction because of his actions, and this cannot be allowed, because it is throwing the entire universe out of balance. Earth is a tiny fragment, but of the greatest importance. It is precious far beyond man's understanding.

I just realised that "evil" is "live" spelled backwards. I never noticed that before. Maybe I've been slow! Do people generally know this? Does it work for other languages?

To live in the full sense of the word is to love. Evil is a corruption of love and life. Those who commit to evil are living backwards. They have turned from the light.

All your languages are full of codes and hidden meanings. As you know, there are other languages than those which are spoken, such as art, mathematics and music. They are also connected to divine source. They are expressions and interpretations of the divine.

Yes, there are patterns in everything.

The patterns carry the imprint of the divine, and are there as a reflection of the divine.

What do you mean by "divine"? Do you mean God?

Yes.

Where is God?

Everywhere.

Thank you. Who spoke, please?

Uriel.

***

Although I'm beginning to understand this, and to act on it, it seems that the evil in the world is escalating, and examples of cruelty, greed, neglect, ignorance, disrespect and so on can be seen all around. For example, when I look out of the window I see the river, which is always beautiful, but I often see litter on the river bank, or even chunks of plastic floating along, and this seems to be an example of people's disrespect for their environment. In the wider world, the media feed us with news of violence and murder close to home, whilst coverage of the bigger picture is of evil, such as wars and starvation.

You are all connected, to each other and to your environment. You are all affected, and feel the effects of abuse and evil. So now many of you, through your prayers, are asking for forgiveness, for yourself and for those to whom you have been connected. You free yourselves, and help the Earth to heal also. You are more sensitive to the darkness all around, and to acts of evil, but you free yourself, and in so doing you pull others with you, so they may do the same. You shine your lights for others to see by and purify. All is well. You see beauty; you see ugliness and feel the pain of the abuse of your world and its people. There is more work to do. Keep shining the light. Notice the litter, the ignorance and the abuse, which are all evil, and do what you can, but despair not. For we tell you that the world is healing fast, and all will pass. Everything will be healed, or will self-destruct.

May I ask, what is beauty?

Beauty is a portal through which you see God, through which you feel God, or through which you hear God. Beauty is recognised by your heart, and when your heart rejoices the angels rejoice with you, for you have recognised the hand of God, or the touch of God, or the feeling of God. Beauty comes to you through your senses. Beauty is the imprint of God in your physical dimension. Beauty therefore connects you to the divine.

If one person picks up litter in a beautiful place and another throws it down, or if someone trashes his environment where someone else enriches it, what does this mean?

It means that one person recognises beauty where another does not. Furthermore, the one who recognises has beauty in his soul and responds with gratitude, whereas the other has beauty in his soul and responds with pain or anger. This is because the impression he receives from the outside does not match the feelings of self-worth he has within him.

May I ask, if children were not taught anything about litter or cleaning up, would they trash things and leave mess everywhere?

We tell you that a child would not trash who has a heart to feel, eyes to see and ears to hear the essence of the divine.

What about small children who crush spiders on windowsills? I even seem to remember chopping wasps in half with rulers when I was in primary school, whereas now I can't kill anything – except midges, perhaps, when they bite.

This is all learned behaviour. Killing for food with respect for the source which has provided and for the animal which offers its meat is one thing, and killing for sport is another. One is done with a spirit of thanksgiving and the other through cruelty. Cruelty is learned behaviour. You learned not to kill for pleasure because of the negative feelings it aroused within you, which caused you to change. When these negative feelings become numbed in a person, he does not know he has done wrong because he cannot feel. He needs to be guided with compassion.

***

79

I thought I was an ordinary woman living in Scotland, a single parent, with the worries of all parents, such as wanting my children to be happy and to have the opportunities they deserve in education and future careers, and worries about how I can finance the lifestyle I wish for. I long for the health to be able to live a normal life, and to continue to offer my services in art teaching to those who might benefit from my experience. I fear sometimes for my future, in terms of both health and wealth.

Why have you chosen me to be your scribe? Why didn't you choose someone more confident than me to promote your teachings? I don't know how on earth I can write your book. If I were a clever person, I'd know what questions to ask, and which arguments and philosophies to bring to it. It would surely be so much better to ask someone with more brain than me. It seems such a wasted opportunity to be asking me!

Dear child, you have been chosen for this task. You are the right person for this task. You are intelligent, and more importantly you feel deeply the power of God, recognise beauty, and have an acute awareness of the divine in all things. You have suffered much pain and illness but have come through this because of your faith. Many who are to read this will be coming from the experience of suffering and pain, and will be able to identify with what we have been telling you. It is because you have walked this path, and also have the ability to record our words, and to ask us questions from your human perspective, that we have chosen you. You are the right person to scribe for us. You need to trust more. You need to believe in yourself. This you will learn. Ask no more. Question no more. We beseech you to trust. You are chosen for this task, so believe it. Again we say to you, believe it. Believe us. You are greatly loved.

We are happy with what you have written. You can hear us clearly at times.

I'm glad, because I don't know how accurate I'm being.

It is fine. We are in charge of this but you have taken down our words faithfully, and we wish that you learn to touch-type!

Thank you, Angels.

Chapter 8

The Importance of Spirituality

Dear Angels,

I find myself here again after another long gap. I have feared writing your book. I'm here to continue.

I have no question to ask today. Please guide me. Please speak to me.

You have been urgently called to be here today. It is time to continue writing.

You can see how much is changing in your world, even in the past few months. There are great changes taking place in the spiritual dimension, and this in turn is affecting all that happens in the physical realms. Whilst great healings are taking place in the lives of people – we mean, in their personal lives – there are also healings of spirit. This then affects everything else connected to the source of the healing person. There are waves of healing. People are having to purify their thoughts to keep up with the vibration which is around them, and when thoughts are purified, then actions become more consistent with the truth which each person represents. It is becoming harder for people not to act out of truth. At the same time, the forces of evil are making a counter-attack, because of the movement of so many towards goodness and truth. So many are turning to the light, and evil itself is threatened. There is a massive counter-attack. So it seems in your world as if acts of cruelty, vengeance, greed and so on have reached a scale which has never been seen before. We have to remind you that it is because of the increasing light in your world that the acts of evil are shown up as never before. The light is always greater than the darkness, and the darkness has nowhere left to hide, as it were, and so it shows up in its most awful aspect.

We hear you thinking, "How could this be done to a child, to this or that innocent person?" Evil knows no bounds. Goodness knows no bounds. Goodness is greater. Those who are acting from their hearts are truly powerful, and have the ability to remove much of the evil from a situation.

Prayer is most powerful at this time. Send white light continuously if you can, and surround yourself and those you love with the light to protect them. Darkness cannot compete.

Many of you have been removing evil from situations throughout your life without even knowing it, because every thought you have goes out. If it is a true thought with its basis in love or goodness, then it will have an effect on people and in places far removed from the origin of the thought. You are all senders and receivers. When people become misaligned with their source, then effect continues down a false path, and bad things start to happen.

I'm a bit confused by what you say, because I thought we were not judged by our thoughts and actions, but were free to think and do as we pleased, and that whatever a person thought or did, he'd be forgiven.

This is true. A person is always forgiven. What we are speaking of are the physical effects of a person becoming disconnected from source. The person concerned may have "fallen" into misalignment through the circumstances of his life, or through the example of others who have misled him, mistreated him, tempted him, deliberately deceived or threatened him, or in some other way forced him to move in a direction contrary to his belief. Illness or great hardship can also weaken a soul and make a person more vulnerable to being misled. Ultimately all is forgiven, but acts of abuse, cruelty, greed, oppression and so on only proliferate if there are victims who allow this kind of manipulation, or are caught up in some grand manifestation of these cycles, such as war or famine. Now there are so many who are refusing to comply that there is a shift taking place. People are consciously choosing to go towards the light, because they are choosing to follow their hearts. Or they are consciously choosing to ignore the promptings of their hearts, and to continue in the old patterns of abuse.

In past times, people recognised this kind of choice as being a spiritual choice, as a choice to believe or not to believe.

People did not understand that everyone has a connection with the divine, and as you know, your religions, sects and creeds, on either side of this belief or non-belief, are involved in arguing or justifying the reasoning for belief and action. Or inaction.

I'm trying to formulate what you are telling me. There are many questions arising in my mind, but I think the bottom line is this: are you saying that religions don't matter?

We are saying that it matters not where you come from, where you live, or what religion or denomination you belong to. It matters not, if you do not follow the promptings of truth within your heart. It counts for nothing, unless the religion is a vehicle to express that which comes from the heart.

How about if some parts of a religion allow or prompt people to act from their hearts but other parts do not?

You mean that some parts may be controlling and destructive, and other parts creative, but we say it counts for nothing unless the person concerned is acting from his heart, and not knowingly buying into any deceit.

I have to say, I'm a bit shocked, because you are angels, and I expected angels to abound in any Church or denomination.

Indeed, we do! But you must understand that it is not the energy of manipulation and control that draws us, but the energy created by people who have thought pure thoughts. And we abound in places where prayers have been uttered, and where our help has been desired and sought. In churches, the thought-forms resonate with the prayers of people who have prayed from their hearts. The structure of the system that created the opportunity for people to come to these places does not count. It is the living prayer, the living vibration of true prayer, and the request for help from spirit that draws us there.

***

I'm back again with more thoughts arising from this question of religions. I have many friends who belong to this or that denomination in Scotland. I have friends with strong beliefs who align themselves with particular denominations. I also have friends who hold no such religious beliefs. I don't think it matters to me what the beliefs are – it's rather a question of their friendship and love towards me. However, I think I'll be very afraid when they find out through this book that I claim to be communicating with angels.

What are you afraid of? We think you are afraid of claiming to be "better than" the next person because you have been given this task to take down our communications.

I think that, deep in my heart, I know this is all true, and that this is really happening to me, but that I might somehow be punished, rejected, ridiculed or thought to be mentally ill or unbalanced because of it. And I'm sorry to sound so negative, but I really am afraid, and there seems no point in not coming out with this, as you know my thoughts in any case!

You have to trust us when we tell you that anyone who opens

this book and reads the words herein knows that what you are scribing is the truth from God, as delivered to you from angels, and accepted by you because you have had the openness and courage to follow this call. You have to accept now that you have the ability to commune with us, your angels. When you can fully accept this, then others also will fully accept it. It is a blessing. Do not make it a burden on yourself. Do not be so hard on yourself.

You have been persecuted in past lives for your perception and faith. It is not easy to rid the fear which comes from this awareness of the past. However, it is time to let it go and move forward. We are all moving forward into glorious times when Heaven and Earth shall be as one.

All is sacred. We rejoice.

I need to come back to this subject of religions again. You speak of past lives. I know that belief in past lives is not generally accepted in "western" religions, such as Christianity, whereas I think angels are generally accepted in most religions. Yet you speak of past lives and karma, and it seems fundamental to the explanation of many things you speak of in this book. A lot of people will not be able to accept the idea of past lives and karma.

That is their choice. We do not require that people believe in angels, or in past lives and karma. We do not require that people believe in anything. It is their choice. If they are reading this, it is their choice. If they do not choose to pick up this book, then that is their choice.

Heaven is infinite, and you can only glimpse it to the extent that you believe. If you have no belief, then you do not see anything. You say, "seeing is believing", but as far as we are concerned, "believing is seeing". You do not have to see, feel or know we are here to believe we are here. Trust is all.

Thank you, Angels.

Chapter 9

Beauty

Dear Angels,

For months I've had come into my head a painting by the fifteenth-century Italian artist Domenico Ghirlandaio, a portrait of an old man and a young boy. Every time I want to ask you about beauty, this painting swims into my mind. Are you asking me to represent it here?

Yes, we are glad you have mentioned this at last. We have been waiting for you to ask.

Please describe or show this image in the book.

This painting by Domenico Ghirlandaio from c.1490 is in the Louvre, Paris. (It can be viewed easily online by searching for the artist's name together with the painting title – either "Old Man with His Grandson" or "Old Man with a Young Boy".)

The artist was renowned in his time for his large-scale figure scenes, painted with technical virtuosity in every detail and earning him commissions from the Florentine aristocracy.

In this double portrait, Ghirlandaio adopted innovations from Flemish art, showing the main figure in three-quarters profile and lit from a window, thus creating a powerful illusion of reality.

Both the old man and the boy are dressed in rich clothes, the orange red of the fabric contrasting starkly with the grey marble background of the window surround. The light from the window falls across the old man's face and highlights his grossly disfigured nose, painted with such accuracy that his condition has been identified as rhinophyma acne rosacea. The boy's face, seen in profile, framed with gold curls flowing from under his cap, is perfect and cherubic by comparison. The old man looks lovingly downwards at this young child in his arms, leaning against him with outstretched arm, and gazing upwards adoringly and wonderingly, straight towards the old man's nose. The window view behind them shows road and river winding through a landscape towards a rocky mountain outcrop.

The painting is striking in every detail of cloth, skin, hair and facial expression, but the loving gaze between the old man and the child, strongly uniting them, gives a sense that we are looking in on their relationship, as much as at any painted detail.

We understand that your choice would have been a painting by the artist Vermeer, and we acknowledge his ability to paint the divine light, and to imbue every object with this light, so that it appears in paint as it does in life to those who can see that light.

Here we give you this image as a picture about beauty. The image has been recognised over the centuries as a great work of art, of which there are many. This painting was not intended by the artist as one of his greatest. Technically and in terms of size and scale, and output, he was able to astonish, of course, but this painting needs no explanation. The recognition of its worth is from those who see it rather than those who know anything about history or art. The identity of the figures in the painting, though they were rich and well known in their time, is lost. The true purpose of the painting – to show the beauty of the connection between the child and his grandfather – is there forever.

You can recognise through your heart that there is great love there. Most people can recognise love when they see it. We said before that beauty is a portal through which the divine is accessed. Some see it, some hear it, some feel it, and some know it.

Love transforms and heals, and the love of the grandfather envelops the child, and empowers him. The love of the child also empowers the grandfather – the child sees only the beauty, and therefore the grandfather's face is beautiful. The painting does not allow you to escape this truth. You might have expected that the child's face would contrast with that of the old man. Beauty reveals truth. The souls of these people are full of love.

You are seen by God as perfect. You are seen with eyes of love.

Therefore forgive yourselves, because God sees you as perfect, and why would you think you had a better idea of perfection than God? You look outside for beauty. It is everywhere. It is nowhere. It is within. It is within your soul and connects you to the divine. It is recognition. You recognise it through your senses.

What is ugliness?

Ugliness is beauty corrupted, as evil is a corruption of the power of love.

Is ugliness sin, then?

We would say to you that ugliness is created by the denial of or refusal to recognise beauty. It is created in ignorance of beauty. Recognition is the awareness.

You were all gifted with your senses. You all have the ability to follow your awareness. When you follow your awareness you discover truth. Beauty reveals truth.

We have no more to say on this.

Thank you, Angels.

Chapter 10

Trust, the Doors Are Opening

Dear Angels,

Christmas 2008 – what would you wish to say?

This is the time which has been prophesied. You are blessed to be on Earth in these times. Salvation is happening heart by heart and soul by soul.

The time is here when the light of people on Earth shines so brightly that it casts out much fear and darkness. Everyone has a role to play, in life and in death even. Everyone has a choice – to follow his heart, or to go to darkness, and live in fear.

Fear is all around at this time, and rises to challenge you all. You must face your fears, and choose your path forward. When you choose to be in light, then the angels connect with you, and are there to help you every step of the way.

If you choose to turn away from the light, then you are choosing to perish with all that is old and which no longer serves any purpose here. Fear eats and destroys itself. It cannot survive, and anything based on fear has to perish therefore.

There is great suffering in the world in which you live today. We angels hear the cry from the heart of many of God's children. It is a time of death and rebirth.

This is the prophecy which was heralded by Christ. His life was a picture, an example, of what could be achieved on Earth by one human with the soul of God. But now you must all live as Christ. You must all make the choice to live by the heart – work from the heart. There is no more time allowed for lies, greed and corruption. Each one must make a choice. Choose the path to light, and you choose life.

The old world will die, and with it all who still believe in the old ways.

A new world rises from the dust, peopled by children of God. There will be a new Heaven and a new Earth.

At Christmas, in the Christian tradition at least, we become more aware of depictions of angels – in our churches, in statuary, in stained glass and in paintings. Angels are shown hiding behind organ pipes, in choirs, and emerging from clouds, singing and playing instruments. Do you really play on the harp and sing in choirs?

We sing continually, and we most certainly play any instrument which sounds to a vibration which forms a pattern of harmony in tune with the music of Heaven. We uphold the vibration of the spheres, the vibration of the universe, which is the sound of life itself, and of love. Love and life are vibrations, and music is one form of vibration. We hold this vibration. We are in tune with the vibration of the greater sphere of Heaven, but it is all linked.

The sound of the harp is deeply connected with one aspect of the divine: it is linked with nature – with the vibration of wind and of water.

***

Do you have any message this New Year's Eve 2008?

Many are in fear. It is necessary that those of you who are so able raise your light for others to see by. Your time is come – to lead people to light. It is time to drop fear and burdens, and to dwell in the light. Then you shall be protected, and have nothing to fear.

Your task has been to find a way through forgiveness and healing, and now it is time to show others that path.

Many of you have already been helping others through prayer and by your example. By living from the heart, you are living examples of God's love.

This time will pass, and the new Earth will emerge from the ruins. You are to inhabit this new Earth. Heaven rejoices. All is well.

Do you wish to speak further?

We rejoice. Gratitude is lifting the Earth's vibration to a higher dimension. We have said that gratitude is a gateway to the divine, and it is through gratitude felt by human hearts that the changes are taking place. Gratitude is never a duty, as is taught to children by so many parents and teachers. Gratitude is a natural response in recognition of the gift of life.

Gratitude is freely given, and the returns of joy and abundance are multiplied. Those who are grateful for the life they have will receive abundance on every level. Ingratitude, which comes from fear and lack of awareness, creates poverty on every level.

We spoke of appreciation and love as being on the same level – on the level which connects with the divine aspect of all things. We spoke of joy as a reward which creates further gratitude, further abundance and further joy.

You can only feel joy to the extent that your heart allows. As you open your hearts to love, your hearts receive more. If you close your hearts, your hearts receive less.

Gratitude is a gateway that allows the human mind to access the higher realms and dwell therein. Forgiveness is the key, gratitude is the gateway, trust is the way through the door, and light, love and joy are the reward.

When we say "reward", we do not mean it in the sense of a sweet given to a child as bribery, and we do not expect thanks in the way some misguided parent would force a child to give thanks. To truly give is to give freely, expecting no reward.

To give thanks is a response to life, which is a response only. However, all actions create reactions, all causes create effects, and love and joy are the reward given to those who give freely.

This process opens the heart of the recipient, and creates more love and joy. This then affects that person's actions towards all others, and indeed towards all life, which in turn creates further good.

You ask if evil works the same way. Evil works through the vehicle of fear. Fear is contagious. Fear moves through everyone and everything, until the process is stopped and blocked by some entity or person who is so full of light that the fear cannot touch him.

So you see that it is necessary for each and every one of you who is working for a better world, and even to be able to exist in these new times, to eradicate fear. This is why we have all along been telling you to cast out fear. There is no more room for fear.

This is why you are working on fear, and learning to cast it out. You are paving the way for others to do the same. In so doing you are breaking the links through which fear runs and spreads. This takes courage from the heart, in its true sense.

Many of you are breaking the chains which have bound you to the past, and to patterns which have been destructive through many generations.

Forgiveness is the key to making this change, and courage is necessary. Then you will arrive at the gateway, and pass through the door, to love and light. When you are fully living in the light, you shall fear no more.

May I ask you to pause for a moment, to check that you aren't talking about death here? Many people refer to death in terms of going through a gateway to light on the other side. In fact I experienced seeing that myself, when I had what would commonly be described as a near-death experience.

We hear you, and we understand what you describe.

You must try to understand that everything you are experiencing in your life on Earth is illusion, and that all you see there is a picture which reflects something greater. Beyond your world of illusion is the reality.

You often have glimpses of the reality beyond your everyday circumstances. The "near-death" experience is one such example. In this example you are "shown" symbols which you can interpret, such as the gateway and the door.

Only the light is real. Only love is real. All else is illusion, which has been created, and which acts as a veil between you and what lies beyond.

Some people are seeing clearly beyond this veil. Others, like yourself, have only glimpses. You know what we speak of. Those who have had a spiritual experience will either reject it or accept it. If they accept it, they know that this experience is real, and has come from the reality beyond. If they reject it, it is because they are unable at that time to accept it.

So are you saying that they can't equate the reality with the illusion of the life in which they live?

Perhaps it would be more accurate to say that they cannot equate the reality with the illusion of what they see and understand.

We said earlier that believing is seeing, even though your common saying puts it the other way round. Many want to "see" the evidence, as it were. Some see the reality. Some hear it, some feel it – as you do, dear child – and some know it.

The world in which you are living is being created by your actions and the actions of those to whom you are connected.

"Transformers" are needed to change energy from one level to another, higher level, as you know. People are acting as transformers to shift the level of energy to a higher form, which is in alignment with the divine. You are a transformer, along with some others. That is why you are called to write this book, and why you have suffered much physical pain in your life.

You raised your light, and this caused turbulence in your physical body. You learned to adjust to this new level of being. Your soul chose not to take the opportunity to die in this life, but to transform, and stay in the same life. We are asking you, through this book, to show others how to do this. If they do not transform, through forgiveness and healing, they will not survive on this Earth.

To answer your earlier question, we do not speak of going through the door of trust to the light beyond in order to die, but in order to live.

But, dear Angels, that in itself could be taken to mean "eternal life" as a metaphor for death.

We laugh! There is no such thing as death. Death is a "passage" (and we know you now laugh at our terminology concerning exits and doorways).

Believe us when we tell you that death as you understand it is the transition of the soul from one form to another, and from one life to another.

When we speak of "going through the door" in the context of this book, we are speaking of making this transition whilst remaining in your current life. You may live out this life, and exit, through death, as you understand it, to another life. However, we are talking about changes people are making on Earth, in their lives.

It is happening fast, and you are seeing the changes.

I now understand much more of what you're explaining than when I started this book. Please shine your light on us all, and help us to forgive each other and ourselves, and to follow our hearts with courage.

So be it. Our radiance is upon you. We love you all and wish you happiness always.

Thank you, Angels.

Chapter 11

More on Trust

Dear Angels,

I'm returning to the question of trust after almost three years! I think I've now almost finished the book, apart from dealing with this question. I'm aware that the issue I'm working on in my own life is learning to trust, and I think it's the reason I couldn't hear your answer before! Will you speak again about trust? Is there more to be revealed to me?*

We laugh uproariously. Leave this "interruption" in the book. It is our way of teaching you about trust. You had to leave this issue until last. You had to learn through life itself. The events which are happening to you, such as your healing and happiness, are dependent on your trust.

I see that now!

Faith is necessary to believing that trust is intact, and like an archaeologist with faith as his spade, a person must carefully dig deep to find his trust again under so much rubble of the ages. It can be found by asking to be forgiven, and for help to forgive all who have held you back, and also yourselves. There has to be a letting go. Forgiving is letting go. This includes letting go of ego-based thoughts, and letting go of the desires of the ego, which you have thought necessary to protect yourself.

Now you are coming to understand that your true self is more

* See Chapter 4, p. 47

than your ego. Your true self is motivated by the power of your heart, which connects you to divine love.

This is why it was said that he who gives up his life will find it. We tell you that this is true not only of those who die in the name of love and light and God, but of those who are giving up their life to that power, as they are living their lives.

You have learned in your past, before you incarnated on Earth, that you have trust. That is why a baby or a young child trusts, and we rejoice.

Learn to be as the child who trusts, even though you have been through events which have caused you to forget how to trust. Keep the wisdom you have learned, but throw out the fear.

Dig deep.

We use the metaphor of the archaeologist because we refer to a search that may require the healing of lives before the life you now have. In other words, it may be appropriate to heal past lives in order to find the trust again.

We say to you that all is to be healed for the Earth to survive this time, and the peoples thereon. And all life.

As people are coming into alignment with their spiritual nature, they are forgiving and healing themselves, and as a result not only their current life is healed but also their past lives. Karma is being healed. This has not happened in past times, when only the current life a person lived could be healed. Now it has come to pass that all is healing. This is necessary in these times. There is little time left.

The world is healed heart by heart and soul by soul. It is through your hearts that you are connected to the power of love and life and to all other people, the Earth and all that dwells thereon, and all that lives by that power.

So to fully trust we must find the courage in our hearts?

That is how you connect.

Thank you for revealing this to me. I'm so delighted to see the finished message.

***

How do I trust – how do I get from having feelings of worry churning and burning inside me to feelings of peace and well-being, and the knowledge that all is working for the best outcome? I haven't mastered this yet! Especially when waiting for something to happen in a situation involving a person to whom I'm connected, especially someone I love. If I wanted to learn it in one day, what would you say?

Dear child, we understand you. First, it is necessary to believe that you are creating your outcomes. Worry creates more of the same. Positive outcomes create more of the same. It is a belief system. Even if you understand this with your mind, your old belief system has created habits, and these must be changed.

Change the habit first and the belief will change to match. So we are saying that it would be hard to change the belief mentally, by willing change from the mind. This never works well.

You have come to the understanding that you have to change to be able to manifest the outcomes you desire, which come from love and peace, rather than from a place of worry.

Invoke our help, and create a state of happiness for yourself. Even if it feels a bit false at first, it will start to pull the positive thoughts in with it. Work from the heart, and ask for your heart to be filled with light.

Once you see that this is working, you will have the confidence to repeat the process. One day, it will become completely natural. Then you will be fully trusting, and you will always attract the best outcomes, or be able to reverse unwanted manifestations.

Is it similar then to what you've advised about a person who's in a depressive state?

It is exactly the same.

Can I go back to the point you made about worry creating more of the same, and positive outcomes creating more of the same? I can see that this will work for me, because events are mirrored back to me as I put out my thoughts, but if there's someone else involved, how is the positive outcome created? For example, if my children were out late, and hadn't left me a message even though they'd said they would, I might have to make the decision not to worry but to imagine them safely home, or getting in touch. But if something is happening to prevent them – if they've got into trouble in some way – how is the outcome to stay positive? I can send light to the situation, but I can't control what they're thinking or doing. It would be similar in any situation of waiting for some result on which I feel my happiness or future depends but in which others are involved. How do I keep things working to a positive outcome?

As you said, you need to keep sending light to the situation, and to keep your thoughts positive. If the other people are close to you, you may call on their angels to protect and guide them. Even if they are not close to you, you may call on your angels to intercede with theirs to protect and guide them to the best outcome.

This will greatly help, and if they are thinking negatively and creating problems to impede their desired outcome, the problems can be shifted, and a solution found. This will happen through the power of light, or through their angel.

However, if the undesired outcome (from your perspective) is part of a lesson they have created for their soul's progress, then it may not be stopped, because it is their karma, or simply a lesson they need to learn in this life to create a better future ultimately.

In this case, your help through positive thoughts may cut short or lessen the disagreeable effects of the outcome. In the end, everything will come together for good in right timing, for that person and for yourself.

This is an important point, and it is why we are asking you to pray for each other and send out light continually if you can. There is little time to play out future karma. All those who wish to live on Earth in happiness are having to heal their problems, and find good solutions now.

You have told me about sending out light and staying positive, in order to trust. I'd set myself the task of learning this in one day – yesterday! It started out well, but I ran into problems. I was waiting for news from someone close to me, then the car began to break down and I was lucky to get home. I thought I'd been doing well on the trust, but I then started envisaging garage bills and my friend being in trouble, and I panicked, and found it very hard to raise myself back into the light! If there are very strong emotions around these kinds of worries, then I find it so very hard to get back out of the fear, just as if I'm depressed or ill or in pain it's difficult to imagine happiness and positive outcomes. Do you have any further guidance on how to get out of these negative emotions?

Call on us for strength, and give your problems to us. Know that although you are not feeling good now, you will soon be feeling good. Picture yourself, as in a photograph, with a smile on your face in the knowledge that things will resolve.

So, in effect, you're saying that we need to imagine the best outcome, and that by picturing the resolution first, we create the accompanying feeling of happiness and gratitude. However difficult the situation, or however bad we may feel, we can do this. If we feel we don't have the strength, we can call on your help, to bring love and light for that resolution.

Everything will resolve. The universe is in support of life and is founded on love. Fear and negative happenings come from misalignment in some way. It happens when thoughts turn from love to fear. Events occur as a result, and things will get worse until someone comes along to change the pattern. This creates a knock-on effect, and other events come back into their natural alignment.

Your prayers go out, and even if you do not know exactly where they go, they will arrive and help change events. You are all connected, and your consciousness is connected with all that is happening in your world. Prayers therefore affect everything.

This is why we desire to help you with all your problems on whatever scale, however small. The energy which resolves the small issues is the same as that which resolves the big issues.

The world is saved, heart by heart and soul by soul. Large government initiatives which coerce people into action have a negligible effect now. The power comes from the individual. The power is love. Love is the only power. Love does not coerce.

Thank you, Angels.

Chapter 12

And Finally

Dear Angels,

I'd like to ask you more about fear. You've said that it's illusion and can be cast out, and that this process is necessary if we are to be healed and happy and fully able to live by the power of love as it flows through our hearts.

I heard a man interviewed on the radio who said he has no fear. He said he has so much love in his heart that there is no fear. He's able to go into war zones and places where people are tortured and still have no fear, even when he's in potential danger.

I also heard an interview with an elderly lady who as a young woman had helped to shelter Jews during World War II. She said she'd known she had a fifty per cent chance of not being discovered and had focussed on that fifty per cent. When asked what she would have done if caught, she merely said she would have thought of something, and believed she may have been able to somehow get away with it.

I marvel at these people. I know that when I walk into the doctor's surgery the very thought of being checked can send my blood pressure and heart rate up. I can exhibit the symptoms of real fear as easily as that.

How can I cast out fear, at will?

We laugh!

You understand that fear is illusion, yet you still exhibit the symptoms of fear. We hasten to add, however, that this will only happen in the areas which have not yet been fully healed in a person's psyche. There are exceptional people who can look death in the face and laugh. They can look pain in the face and laugh. They have healed these fears in other lives, in other times, or may not have encountered any experiences which taught them to fear in the first place. If you put a baby in a dangerous situation it may not show fear, because it has not yet been conditioned to do so. And if you put a hero in a torture chamber he may die of fright only when he notices a spider!

You're having me on!

We do not jest! We are showing you that it is all relative. You need to heal the fear at the level at which it has manifested in your own life, without comparing yourself to others. Their lives are theirs. Their problems are for them to solve.

You are forgiven for fearing pain and death, and for fearing an insect, and you are never judged in terms of the importance of the situation which gives you the fear. It is all the same. It is your mind that runs on your imagination to make the fear grow. It is your mind that imagines the most dreadful outcome, which in turn proliferates the fear of the dreadful outcome. The person sitting in the torture chamber may have the ability, through his imagination, to turn his situation around and visualise his release unharmed. The person who fears the doctor's result may visualise the outcome with perfect normal readings. It is the fear of the worst outcome that brings on the symptoms, in the doctor's surgery and in the situation of being caught by those who would torture and kill.

We must bring to your attention that the woman who said she'd focussed on the fifty per cent chance of not being caught was not caught.

The man who could freely visit the war zone and torture chamber was there not because he was caught, but because he went there to help people. The focus of being there to help, in both situations, created the outcome. Both these people are alive and still "helping". The success quality they may have in dealing with fear is perhaps not as you believe.

They did not do these things to test how brave they could be or how much they were prepared to suffer. They were motivated to help people in evil situations. They were acting from the power of love, which overcomes fear. This power gave them the confidence to act without even thinking of any consequences. Fear was not their "issue".

I've heard of other people in situations where they were literally given the physical strength to lift or move something or someone, a strength which wouldn't have seemed possible before or afterwards. I think I've experienced something like that myself. It's a feeling of true power and success.

Sometimes angels lift or carry something physically, or help humans to do so. We also speak of "lifting" in a metaphorical way. Energy from love is light and from evil is heavy. When you move from illness, depression and negativity to happiness and health, your body "feels" lighter. The energy of thought is light, but attracts to a person – through imagination – his experiences. These may be felt in the physical body as light, if they are experiences of happiness and love, or heavy if they are negative and unhappy experiences.

So a person who is caught up in an evil situation – who has been incarcerated, and is in fear of his life – is in that situation because of the energies he has previously attracted to himself through thought. He has to live out the consequences, and may be given the chance to change his situation for the better. If that does not happen, he may be given the chance again in a different life. If he can raise his light, as it were, he may survive to continue in his current life.

You are getting to the heart of this book now.

I need to go back to the question of the relevance of fear in a situation.

I think I asked you the wrong question, because I believed that the example of someone facing potential death was an example of fear that everyone would be able to relate to.

Yes, this is true, but you picked examples of people whose issues happened to be more important than fear of death.

You often confuse fear of life with fear of death. You fear you will die before you have reached your full potential. You fear to live.

People fear to live, fear to love, fear to throw themselves into the joy of being in the moment of trust, of truth, of love and light, which gives them their happiest outcome, their success, their relationship of joy to all that *is*, and their prosperity.

So, trust and fear are linked, then?

We tell you that when you trust life, and trust yourself to live your life, and to love your life, to love others and most importantly to love yourself (so that you can allow yourself to "go for it"), then fear is cast out. The true purpose of fear is to get you physically out of danger, but as we said before, when it is brought to mind, through the power of your imagination, which is working from fear, then fear corrupts, and causes problems in your physical body.

So we ask you how it was when you were on the mountain at night. What were you feeling then?

I know the situation to which you refer. Yes, I was out in the Cairngorm mountains six years ago now, "doing the Big Four" – four Munros in a day. My walking companion became ill halfway, having to stop frequently, and we ended up after twelve hours' walking, still on the summit of one of the mountains.

I didn't feel any fear. I think I'd say that I felt awe. It was so beautiful on the mountain at night. I felt a part of it all, and had no fear of dying up there. But part of me wanted to make sure I would get home to my children, and I was praying to have the strength to make it back before the Mountain Rescue came looking for us.

I was exhausted, but my senses became sharpened, as if I could hear and see much more clearly, even though it became quite dark. I felt empowered. It was almost a feeling of joy and homecoming, I remember. But I love those kinds of situations. I'd rather be on the mountain than in the doctor's surgery any day – or night.

You were trusting, because it was the only thing left to do. When you trust, you do not fear. Fear was being channelled into your physical body for its correct purpose – to sharpen your senses, to help you physically to get out of any danger.

You were helping us – I know that now. I didn't know so much about you then, but I did pray for my friend, and months later she told me that she'd suddenly felt the strength to keep going exactly at that point on the hillside. We also discovered that another close friend of hers had become aware of her distress, psychically, and had started praying for her at that same moment. I was carrying her pack as well as mine, and I'm now amazed that I had the strength to do that. At the time, I was telling her where to put her feet, step by step up the rocks of Carn Toul. You often tell me that you are helping every step of the way! I think that's what I was doing for her, with divine help.

Fear does not exist outside the mind. It can be brought forth through your imagination, and cast out the same way. By using your imagination, and calling forth the courage from your heart, and calling forth the power of love and light, you can cast out fear itself.

Love dispels fear. Light dispels dark. Laughter dispels sorrow, and shakes fear out. There is a power of love, greater than you can ever imagine, and you can call on it to help you in your life. This power is over all. It is the power that has sent you out on your journey through the ages, and that calls you home. You are called home, to live in the light and power. The name of that power is love.

Is there to be a final chapter on love?

There is no need for a final chapter on love. There is no need to explain love. Love is over all, and is what you are made of. You know about love. It is in your heart and in your soul.

When you have turned from the path of love, when you are misguided by fear, when you forget to trust, when you falter and fall, then call on that power, which is there inside you.

There was never any need to go in search of love. It was there inside you. As you learn to come back into alignment with the power of light and love, the same power which operates throughout your world and universe, then you will be living in that power.

When you have cast out fear, you are in the power, and the power is within you enabling you to cast out fear.

When you have learned the way, the way is revealed. Hold high your light for others to see by, and pray for one another. Send light and love and call on us.

The world is healed, and we rejoice.

Is this it?

We smile. You have finished this book.

I'm so happy and grateful to have been given this wonderful experience, and I pray you will stay with me and help us further.

You will always hear us.

Thank you, Angels!

BOOKS

6th Books investigates the paranormal, supernatural,
explainable or unexplainable. Titles cover everything included
within parapsychology: how to, lifestyles, beliefs, myths,
theories and memoir.